By Allan Zullo

SCHOLASTIC INC.

To David and Alecia Wartowski,
whose passionate beliefs about equality, justice, and
fairness have fueled their dedication to helping
improve the lives of others

— A. Z.

No part of this publication may be reproduced, stored in a
retrieval system, or transmitted in any form, or by any means,
electronic, mechanical, photocopying, recording, or otherwise,
without written permission of the publisher.
For information regarding permission, write to Scholastic Inc.,
Attention: Permissions Department,
557 Broadway, New York, NY 10012.

ISBN 978-0-545-76974-7

12 11 10 9 8 7 6 5 4   18 19 20/0

Printed in the U.S.A.   40
First edition, January 2015

ACKNOWLEDGMENTS

I wish to thank the real-life heroes featured in the following pages for their willingness to recall details, in personal interviews with me, of the dramatic and sometimes emotional memories of their experiences as teenage foot soldiers of the civil rights movement from decades ago.

This book was made better with the assistance of Bruce Hartford, who created an exceptional online resource — the Civil Rights Movement Veterans website, crmvet.org. This site, which was an invaluable help to me, is an educational tool for students, academics, researchers, and people in general who want to learn more about those activists, white and black, who gave their hearts and souls to the freedom movement in the Deep South in the 1950s and 1960s. In several instances, Bruce made it easier for me to reach some of these heroes for interviews.

My appreciation extends to those who provided me additional information and confirmation of certain facts. They include: Marilyn Hayden, director of the Green McAdoo Cultural Center; Wayne Coleman, head of archives and technology at the Birmingham Civil Rights Institute; Gregory Wilson, history instructor at Lawson State Community College; and Gerald Ensley, senior reporter and columnist at *Tallahassee Democrat*.

AUTHOR'S NOTE

You are about to read ten true stories of courageous African American high school and college students who were the young heroes of the civil rights movement in the Deep South during the turbulent 1950s and 1960s.

The movement required the strong leadership of great men and women such as Dr. Martin Luther King, Jr., Roy Wilkins, Hosea Williams, James Farmer, Bayard Rustin, Rosa Parks, Ella Baker, and Fannie Lou Hamer.

But in many ways, the movement was powered by black youths who displayed unwavering dedication, commitment, and determination. Their bravery in the face of adversity — when they were beaten and bloodied during peaceful demonstrations — left a profound impression on the nation and the world. Through their nonviolent tactics, they were able to frustrate their vicious foes and bring attention to racial inequality, leading to federal laws that banned discrimination.

These are the real heroes, the unsung heroes, the young heroes.

For this book, I read newspaper and magazine accounts, memoirs, and oral histories of those who were on the front lines of the war against injustice. Selecting a representative sample of these gutsy African Americans, I conducted lengthy personal interviews with ten of them and asked them to relive those difficult days. Some found it easy to recall their experiences. Some found it difficult and emotional because of the horrors they and their comrades suffered.

Using real names, dates, and places, the stories are written as factual and truthful versions of their recollections, although the dialogue has been re-created for dramatic effect. Much of what you will read in the following pages is disturbing because that's the way it really happened. It's hard to imagine that anyone, especially young Americans, had to deal with so much cruelty and hatred.

A word of warning: There is a hurtful word — usually uttered by racists — referring to African Americans that is vile, offensive, and degrading. Evolving from the word *Negro*, this poisonous word was used as a verbal sword that stabbed at the hearts of black people during the days of slavery and especially during the civil rights movement. That word is *nigger*.

You will see the racial slur in this book only in the context of what hatemongers called these black heroes. The decision to include the word in the stories was not made lightly. As a white American, I will never fully understand the pain and anguish it brings to African Americans. I have trouble writing the word because it is such a despicable insult that represents centuries of discrimination, oppression, and violence against a particular race.

During my interviews for this book, the heroes often mentioned the word — and other disgusting racial slurs, too — when recounting what bigots called them. I asked my interviewees if they believed I should include the word in their stories in scenes where it had been used in real life. They said yes. They believe it is important for you, the reader, to get an honest understanding of the verbal abuse and hatred that were heaped upon them in their struggle for equal rights. They want you to grasp the terrible impact and destructive power of this word. And they feel their stories should be told as truthfully as possible without sugar-coating the language.

I feel it's my duty to honor their voice, their stories, and their choice. So based on their judgment, which I greatly respect, I included the word in this book. I am aware that some teachers, parents, and students might find it objectionable to see it in print, even though this is historical nonfiction. I hope that any debate about the word's inclusion will not detract from the achievements of these extraordinary and inspiring heroes who, as young African Americans, triumphed over racial injustice.

In many ways, the civil rights movement has not ended. Today, our country still grapples with racism as well as discrimination, intolerance, and inequality.

In dealing with these issues, perhaps we can learn from the experiences of the civil rights foot soldiers, because they understood the importance of the past and how it helped them right some of society's wrongs. As Janice Wesley Kelsey, whose story you'll read, says, "It's [our] responsibility to know history so we don't repeat the mistakes of the past."

— A. Z.

CONTENTS

THE FIGHT FOR FREEDOM

The 1950s and 1960s were defining decades in the civil rights movement in America. Hundreds of discriminatory laws and unjust social customs on the local and state level were abolished, especially in the Deep South. The Civil Rights Act of 1964 and the Voting Rights Act of 1965 were passed by Congress. And racial attitudes began slowly changing for the better.

Much of the credit for these achievements belongs to the courageous black students who carried the torch of freedom when others couldn't.

Too many black adults risked losing their jobs, homes, and even lives for getting actively involved in the movement. So it was left up to the young African Americans to supply the manpower for the fight against oppression, prejudice, and injustice. They organized boycotts, walked picket lines, and conducted sit-ins. They led marches, demonstrations, and protests. They integrated schools, lunch counters, and movie theaters.

But the battle was costly and difficult. They were often bloodied, beaten, arrested, imprisoned, and sometimes murdered. They sacrificed some of the best years of their lives at a time when other kids their age were dancing to rock 'n' roll, hanging out at drive-ins, and going to the movies.

For decades, Southern states relied on laws specifically designed to make black people second-class citizens and deny them any political power. These acts were known as Jim Crow laws, named after a song sung by a popular white theatrical performer in blackface who mocked the ways African Americans sang and danced.

As a result, the South legally justified and enforced segregation — the term used for the separation of whites and blacks — especially in schools, buses, housing, and other places. "Whites-only" and "colored" signs were posted everywhere — water fountains, bathrooms, lunch counters, waiting rooms, stores, restaurants, and even hospital wards. Segregationists said that this "separate but equal" doctrine was good for both races. But the truth was that the public facilities for African Americans were inferior to those for whites, because whites received most of the benefits from the tax money spent by local and state governments.

Southern customs, traditions, and laws decreed that black people had to ride in the back of the bus and were expected to give up their seats when ordered to by white passengers or drivers. They had to enter many restaurants by the back door or get their food only through takeout. They had to buy their shoes and clothes at white-owned stores without being allowed to try on the items. They had to sit in the balcony of movie theaters rather than on the main floor where whites sat. They were routinely denied access to tax-supported public areas such as beaches, swimming pools, parks, and picnic areas.

Black people who tried to register to vote, or speak out against injustice, or violate the racial customs of the South faced the wrath of violent groups such as the Ku Klux Klan. Members were white supremacists — people who believe that the white race is superior to all other races. Clad in white robes and cone-shaped hats that often hid their faces, Klansmen inflicted a reign of terror against black people through cross burnings, drive-by shootings, muggings, kidnappings, and lynchings and other forms of murder.

Many Southern towns were under the thumb of a white citizens' council, which was made up of influential local politicians, businessmen, and even clergymen who were well respected — and also racist. They had the clout, which they often used, to economically ruin anyone — white or black — who fought for racial equality. Because of the councils' power, thousands of black sharecroppers who tried to register to vote were thrown off the land they worked, and sympathetic whites who tried to help them were often run out of town.

However, white supremacists suffered a body blow in 1954 when the United States Supreme Court unanimously ruled in a legal case called *Brown v. Board of Education* that segregation in public schools was unconstitutional. As schools in other areas began integrating, black students of all ages felt the brunt of bigoted backlash. The kids often had to walk through a gauntlet of angry white adults who cursed and spit at them.

Despite facing punishing reprisals, black high school and college students volunteered by the thousands to fight for freedom. They were taught the principles of nonviolent direct action, passive resistance, and peaceful civil disobedience. Supporting them were organizations such as the National Association for the Advancement of Colored People (NAACP); the Congress of Racial Equality (CORE); the Southern Christian Leadership Conference (SCLC), which was led by Rev. Martin Luther King, Jr.; and the Student Nonviolent Coordinating Committee (SNCC, which was pronounced "snick").

In early 1960, four black freshmen from North Carolina Agricultural and Technical State University — Ezell Blair, Jr., Franklin McCain, Joseph McNeil, and David Richmond — began a sit-in at a segregated Woolworth's lunch counter in Greensboro, North Carolina. Their passive, dignified protest — sitting quietly at the lunch counter for hours while being heckled — grew larger every day and triggered boycotts of other stores that had segregated lunch counters. The protests worked. Within six months, the stores began serving people of all races.

Inspired by the Greensboro sit-ins, African American students throughout the South began holding similar nonviolent protests, some more successful than others. Student-led marches, pickets, boycotts, and sit-ins in dozens of towns and cities opened parks, swimming pools, theaters, libraries, lunch counters, and other public facilities to black people. But in other parts of the Deep South, students were clubbed, beaten, tear-gassed, and jailed for peacefully demonstrating. Convicted on mostly phony charges, the students were often sentenced to hard time on prison farms, toiling on road gangs overseen by racist, sadistic guards.

During the summer of 1961, a racially mixed group of students and adults known as Freedom Riders took bus trips through the Deep South to test new federal laws that banned segregation in interstate travel facilities such as bus and train stations. The Riders were met with violence and arrests. By the end of summer, about 1,000 volunteers, black and white, participated in the rides, even though hundreds were arrested and shipped off to prison. Their courage and commitment raised the awareness of white Americans, putting pressure on states and local governments to follow federal law and integrate the facilities.

In 1963, Birmingham, Alabama, was ground zero in the civil rights struggle. Black students from grade school, middle school, and high school participated in protest marches known as the Children's Crusade. More than 700 were arrested the first day. On the second day, a new wave of students was blasted by high-pressure fire hoses, beaten by the cops, and attacked by police dogs. Photos and footage of the mayhem against the defenseless children horrified many Americans and caused them to search their consciences.

Ironically, the students' best weapons proved to be no weapons at all. Because they had adopted nonviolent tactics, the more brutality and cruelty they suffered at the hands of white supremacists, the more support and sympathy they received from the rest of the country.

But violence continued to escalate. On September 15,

four young girls attending Sunday school at Birmingham's Sixteenth Street Baptist Church — where civil rights meetings were often held — were killed when a bomb exploded. The senseless murders ignited riots in the city and calls for stronger federal laws banning segregation.

Just three weeks earlier, in the largest demonstration ever seen in the nation's capital, more than 250,000 people — mostly African Americans — participated in the March on Washington for Jobs and Freedom. It was here where Dr. King delivered his famous "I Have a Dream" speech.

Feeling pressure from the growing protest movement, Congress passed the Civil Rights Act of 1964, which prohibited discrimination of all kinds based on race, color, religion, or national origin.

Even so, areas in the Deep South still resisted change with a vengeance, and bigoted local and state governments tried every means possible to prevent African Americans from registering to vote. During the Freedom Summer of 1964, nearly a thousand civil rights volunteers — many of them students from all races, backgrounds, and regions — fanned out in Mississippi in a campaign to educate and register black voters. They put their lives on the line and, tragically, some lost theirs. Three civil rights workers in their early twenties — two white and one black — were murdered by the KKK.

In Alabama in 1965, where more civil rights supporters were slain, thousands tried to march from Selma to the state capital in Montgomery to push for voting rights. But shortly after they started, the marchers were blocked by a large police force. When demonstrators kneeled down to pray, they were tear-gassed, clubbed, and whipped in what became known as Bloody Sunday.

Once again, the images of police beating defenseless men, women, and children jarred the sensibilities of Americans. Eventually, 25,000 people arrived in Montgomery for an emotional rally. The march and rally helped pave the way for passage of the Voting Rights Act of 1965, which outlawed discriminatory laws and practices that had made it so difficult for African Americans to register.

But with victories came more attacks, imprisonments, and murders. On April 4, 1968, Martin Luther King, Jr., was gunned down in Memphis, Tennessee.

When the decade drew to a close, those young people who sacrificed so much and fought so hard against racial injustice had secured rights not only for themselves but for future generations as well. They helped make America a better, fairer, more just country.

THERESSER CASWELL AND THE CLINTON 12

All Theresser Caswell and 11 other black students tried to do in 1956 was quietly fit in with the white student body at Clinton High School, get an education, and have fun in their teenage years.

They received an education that was much more than just literature, chemistry, and algebra. They learned how hate — directed specifically at them — could turn a town upside down, pit neighbors against neighbors, and twist ignorant minds.

When she was in eighth grade, Theresser (who went by her middle name instead of her first name, Anna) and her family moved to Claxton, Tennessee, which was a few miles from Clinton, a town of 3,700 predominantly white residents. Because African Americans weren't allowed to attend Clinton's only public high school, Theresser assumed that for ninth grade she would go to the closest all-black school, Austin High in Knoxville. Austin was a 45-minute bus ride away and, unlike the white school, required a small tuition.

That was just the way things were for black people in Anderson County. For the most part, there were no racial issues in Clinton — as long as black people knew their place and didn't dare sit in seats on the main floor of the Ritz movie theater, or at the whites-only lunch counter, or at the desks of an all-white school.

In 1950, four black students tried to enroll at Clinton High but were barred by the school board. The students sued. Eventually, District Court Judge Robert Taylor, of Knoxville, ruled against the students. However, in spring 1956 — two years after the United States Supreme Court ruled that segregation in schools was unconstitutional — Taylor reversed himself and ordered the Anderson County school board to accept black students at Clinton High, beginning with the 1956–57 term. The decision meant that Clinton High would become the first state-supported public school in the Deep South to be integrated.

Although most whites in town weren't happy about the ruling, they didn't hold any public protests because of their strong belief in obeying the law of the land. Toward the end of the 1955–56 school term, Clinton High even held classroom discussions and general assemblies to prepare the 700 white students for the dozen African Americans who would be joining them in the fall. Despite their deep-seated reservations, the townspeople seemed committed to making school integration work and put up no resistance when the black students registered for classes at Clinton High in late summer.

Theresser and black students JoAnn Allen, Bobby Cain, Minnie Ann Dickie, Gail Ann Epps, Ronald "Poochie" Hayden, William Latham, Alvah McSwain, Maurice Soles, Robert Thacker, Regina Turner, and Alfred Williams would forever be known as the Clinton 12.

Even though they were about to shatter the "separate but equal" doctrine that had been part of the Southern way of life for decades, Theresser wasn't worried about facing any harassment. In fact, she was looking forward to going to school.

But then white supremacist John Kasper, 26, of Washington, DC, showed up, determined to turn the town into a battleground. His weapon of choice was hate.

As leader of the extremist Seaboard White Citizens' Council — its motto was "Honor-Pride-Fight: Save the White" — he knew that if Clinton High was integrated without a struggle, then it would set a standard that other cities throughout the South would follow. And that was a scenario he just couldn't stomach.

Dressed in a suit and tie, the clean-cut, well-spoken racist held a rally in Clinton, exploiting the townspeople's prejudices and preying on their fears of desegregation. He said that a strong display of opposition would convince officials to ignore federal integration laws. He said, "And if that fails, then we might be forced to resort to more drastic measures." Everyone understood what he meant. They would use violence as a tactic to make black parents afraid to send their children to a white school.

Although Theresser's parents said nothing to her about potential trouble, she now was aware of the possibility. So

3

when she woke up on Monday, August 27, 1956 — the first day of school — she prayed that everything would be all right.

On that history-making morning, the black students met at the nearby all-black Green McAdoo Elementary School. For support and solidarity, they walked together down Foley Hill toward Clinton High. Along the way, they were confronted by several picketers, who held up racist signs and called them names. But the black students ignored the demonstrators, who were outnumbered by reporters, photographers, and cameramen.

Inside the school, Theresser, who was entering as a freshman, felt the tension in the hallways. Most of the white students didn't know how to react to their new black classmates, so they tended to ignore them. In a few cases, a bigoted kid "accidentally" bumped into a black student or uttered a slur or tossed a spitball. But overall, the first day of integration at Clinton High went off without a hitch and made national headlines and the TV news.

The next day turned ominous. Roused by Kasper, dozens of menacing segregationists showed up in front of the school, spewing vicious threats and verbal abuse and waving crude, insulting signs as the black students walked by. Some of the white kids in school took the demonstration as a sign to hassle the Clinton 12 in halls and classrooms.

Working furiously to ignite even greater outrage over integration, Kasper held a rally that drew more than 1,000 people Wednesday night. In a fiery speech, he told them the law on integration didn't need to be obeyed. "The basis of common law is the custom of the people," he said. "And if the custom of the people in Anderson County is to keep the races separate, then the Supreme Court law doesn't mean anything."

By Thursday morning, the Clinton 12 nervously walked past a gauntlet of hundreds of irate townspeople and agitators recruited from other areas. The racists screamed, cursed, and spit at them, and held handwritten signs that read GO HOME, NIGGERS; GO HOME, COONS; KEEP NIGRAS OUT OF CHS.

Inside, the level of harassment increased. Someone glued Theresser's locker shut. In the hallway between classes, a student slapped her on the back of the head before disappearing into the crowd. Other black students discovered that their lockers had been vandalized or marred by crude messages scrawled in ink.

Meanwhile, Judge Taylor issued a temporary restraining order, forbidding Kasper and his followers from interfering with school integration. When Kasper ignored the injunction and continued to stir up trouble, the judge had federal marshals arrest the racist militant for criminal contempt of court.

The arrest did nothing to quell the boiling racial hatred. Asa Carter, a white citizens' council leader from Birmingham, Alabama, rushed in to take Kasper's place and kept passions inflamed with another rally that attracted an estimated 1,500 bigots.

Speaking to a television reporter, Theresser's black schoolmate, JoAnn Allen, said she was disheartened by the growing number of demonstrators. "On Wednesday morning I almost cried because there were so many people, and they looked so mean and looked like they wanted to grab us and throw us out, and they didn't want us at all," she said. "I could see the hate in their hearts. When we got inside of the school, most of the children were very nice to us, but there were some you could tell didn't want us there. They showed it in a big way. They put signs on our lockers that said, 'Get out.' They shoved us in the halls. They threw chalk at us. They said all sorts of nasty things. And it just made me feel bad. I couldn't concentrate at all on my lessons."

Afraid to eat in the school cafeteria, Theresser and her friend Alvah McSwain walked to the county jail, where Alvah's mother worked, and had lunch there the first three days. On the way there on Thursday, Alvah said that she had talked to fellow black student Alfred Williams, who was a senior. "Alfred told me that he's carrying a knife to school," she told Theresser. "He says he can't possibly get anything learned or done, because he's scared that the white kid next to him is planning to kill him."

After returning to school, Theresser was in study hall when a teacher came up to her and said, "Get your books and follow me." Without further explanation, the teacher ushered her out of school through the back door, where she was joined by the other black students. They were told to get into waiting police cars.

"Are we being arrested?" Theresser asked an officer.

He shook his head. Pointing to a crowd of hundreds of incensed people gathering near the school, the officer said, "See all those people out there? They're waitin' for you to come out of school so they can hurt you. We're gettin' y'all out of here."

For the first time since she started classes at Clinton High, Theresser was scared.

The officers took the black students to Green McAdoo. From there, they got rides home or walked with the cops, who made sure the students weren't attacked. Theresser took a school bus, which transported the black elementary-school students, to her house in Claxton.

Outsiders — mostly Ku Klux Klansmen and other white supremacists from the surrounding area — were arriving in Clinton by the hour. Then they began driving up and down the streets, uttering rebel yells, honking horns, and shouting racial epithets from the top of their lungs.

On Friday night, Asa Carter's hate-filled speech whipped nearly 2,000 people into a frenzy. Someone in the crowd fired a pistol in the air, signaling the start of a full-scale riot. The mob overturned cars, smashed windows, and carried out drive-by shootings in the black neighborhoods. Several black soldiers on leave, who happened to be passing through town, barely escaped with their lives after being chased through the streets. Meanwhile, the trouble-makers who had taken over Clinton threatened to blow up the mayor's house, the newspaper office, and even the courthouse.

Because Clinton's seven-man police force was overwhelmed and unable to handle the onslaught of racists, Mayor W. E. Lewallen recruited 47 prominent citizens and made them special deputies to help restore order. They brought along their own rifles, shotguns, and sidearms. Some of the men stood guard outside the homes of white residents who had been threatened with bodily harm by segregationists for supporting — or, at the very least, not fighting against — integration.

On Saturday, September 1, an unruly mob of 1,500 racists had gathered in the square by the courthouse. In front of the building, the armed special deputies formed a straight line shoulder to shoulder and began marching across the square, trying to disperse the crowd. But the deputies were greatly outnumbered.

In the throng, some of the angriest rabble-rousers shouted, "Let's go get them! Let's take their guns away and kill them!"

The deputies retreated into the courthouse and called Governor Frank Clement for help. Although the governor had supported segregated schools, he believed more strongly in law and order and sent in the Tennessee Highway Patrol.

With lights flashing and sirens wailing, about two dozen cruisers paraded once around the besieged courthouse square and stopped. Stepping out of the lead cruiser was the head of the highway patrol, six-foot-eight-inch Greg O'Rear, a double-barreled shotgun resting on his broad shoulder. He stared at the mob and announced in a deep, authoritative voice, "Boys, it's all over."

Within minutes, the people, many of them grumbling, began to leave. The immediate crisis had been defused. But O'Rear knew that it would flare up again unless there was a force stronger than the 100 troopers he had brought with him. So Clement called out the Tennessee National Guard to relieve the officers. The governor also announced that residents in Clinton were under martial law and were banned from gathering in large groups.

On Sunday morning, 600 guardsmen, with bayonets fixed, marched into town to keep the peace. They brought with them several army tanks that were positioned at various intersections.

Every day after school for the next month, Theresser was met outside by armed guardsmen who silently escorted her across the street and waited with her until the school bus of black kids from Green McAdoo arrived to take her to Claxton. Because the rest of the Clinton 12 lived in the black neighborhood atop Foley Hill, they walked together to Green McAdoo with guardsmen by their side.

Theresser had it easier than the others. She found sanctuary at home, which was far from town, where she could forget about her troubles. At the dinner table, her parents and two younger siblings seldom asked how school was, which was fine with her. She didn't want to talk about it, anyway.

But the other black students could never relax in their homes, because their neighborhood was often under attack by racist thugs. Theresser's friend Regina Turner, of the Clinton 12, complained to her, "There's no peace at night."

White supremacists often roared down the streets throwing sticks of lit dynamite or firing guns at the houses of African Americans. One night someone triggered a 55-gallon drum of explosives across from Alvah's house, blowing out her front windows. Sometimes Alvah and her family had to hide at Mount Sinai Baptist Church or at someone else's house because of death threats. Alvah's home was targeted because her parents had filed the original lawsuit against the Anderson County school board back in 1950.

When JoAnn Allen's father was tipped off that armed

Klansmen would be driving down his street, he stood out in the front yard with a loaded gun to protect his family. The cops found out and arrested him, but not the Klansmen.

The intimidation wasn't focused only at the families of the Clinton 12. Crosses were burned on the lawns of certain white faculty members and civic leaders who supported integration. Anonymous phoned death threats were common and often targeted Clinton High's white school principal, D. J. Brittain.

In the hallways and classrooms at the school, the black students lived with constant pestering and bullying from about 50 to 100 whites. Some of the black upperclassmen didn't want to be at Clinton because their friends were attending the all-black Austin High and going to school dances, football games, and after-class clubs. The Clinton 12 weren't able to enjoy any of those school activities.

One day, Theresser asked Brittain if she and other black schoolmates could go to an upcoming nighttime pep rally. The principal replied, "Well, I can't tell you that you can't. I can tell you that it won't be safe if you do. We simply can't protect you." None of the black students went.

To boost the morale of the Clinton 12, sympathetic whites would take them on fun outings on the weekends and hold dances and parties for them. Students at Knoxville College helped tutor those who were having difficulty with their studies. Theresser was getting decent grades, but they suffered under the pressure she was feeling.

As the weeks passed, life for the Clinton 12 in school became more tolerable. Some of the black students had actually made friends with whites. A few white students were pleasant toward Theresser but weren't looking to be her friend. She could tell that some of the teachers wanted to be nice to the African Americans but remained distant out of fear of being badgered by segregationists. However, several brave teachers chose to treat the black students with the same respect given to the white students.

Although racially motivated torment was still a common occurrence, the amount and frequency had eased. That is, until Kasper reentered the picture. After his arrest during the first week of school, he had posted bond and left town. But then he returned in November to face trial on charges of sedition and inciting a riot.

Rather than act contrite for his past abhorrent actions, Kasper used this time to create a junior white citizens' council composed mostly of high school students whose mission was to hound the Clinton 12. They poured ink and dropped rotten eggs in the black students' lockers, put thumbtacks on their seats, hurled their books out windows, and stomped on their feet. Theresser had things thrown at her in class, was shoved against a locker, was called "nigger" constantly, and had her hair pulled. The boys had it much worse, getting punched and kicked in the hallways. To curb the harassment, Brittain enlisted football players to serve as hall monitors and report any problems. But Theresser discovered that a couple of the players were among those causing the trouble.

"There's no way teachers can watch seven hundred kids at one time," Alfred Williams told her one day. "We're just going to have to tolerate the abuse."

One day, Alfred, one of two black seniors, was held after class, which delayed him from walking home with his younger brother, Maurice Soles, who was a freshman. After Alfred was released, he headed up Foley Hill when he spotted a group of knife-wielding white boys circling someone, and he heard them shout, "Cut him! Kill him!"

Drawing closer, Alfred realized the person being threatened was Maurice. Alfred pulled out his knife and ordered the white students to leave his brother alone or face getting slashed. They took off running. The next day at school, Alfred was expelled for carrying a knife, but Maurice's assailants weren't even reprimanded.

The harassment in school soon escalated to such a point that the parents of the black students decided to keep their children out of classes until there were assurances that the school could provide a safe environment for them. (Theresser was already home because she was recovering from foot surgery.) During this time, the town was gearing up for municipal elections between the incumbents and a slate of segregationists who were running on a platform of returning Clinton High to an all-white school.

On December 4, which was Election Day, the black students agreed to return to class. Three white men — Leo Burnett, Sidney Davis, and Rev. Paul Turner of First Baptist Church — escorted them from Green McAdoo, down Foley Hill, past hecklers and into the high school. The men then went their separate ways.

While walking alone toward his church, Turner was brutally attacked by several white men who pummeled him and then left him lying bloody and bruised. Shortly afterward, white thugs entered the school and knocked down Brittain's wife, who was a teacher, and then assaulted several white and black students. Fearing further violence, Brittain closed the entire school at 11:45 A.M. and sent everyone home.

As word of the attacks spread throughout the town, shocked residents swarmed to the polls and voted overwhelmingly to support the current mayor and city councilmen, denying the racist candidates a single victory.

At a quickly arranged PTA meeting to discuss the school's temporary closing, Eleanor Davis, a mother and teacher, told parents, "We teachers were stunned [by the closing]. I found students crying and some seniors who were bitter and afraid they wouldn't be able to graduate. Teachers didn't want to leave, so we went into the faculty room and we felt defeated. We felt we had raised the flag of surrender when we didn't want to raise the flag of surrender."

Mrs. Davis told the audience that the worst behavior didn't occur until Kasper had returned to town and organized a junior white citizens' council. "Members weren't all students, but some of those who were happened to be habitual troublemakers," she said. "Other members had been forced to join by their parents and were so ashamed to be a part of it that they wouldn't wear their badges. They refused to participate in any of the troublemaking. I can't say enough about the courage of the Negro students. They face persecution in their hometown to get an education. Most white students have undergone this with great courage and are trying to be courteous and helpful — and they've grown up because of it."

Within days, authorities arrested two men in connection with the attack on the Tennessee-born, 33-year-old minister, who recovered from his injuries. Federal agents also arrested 16 men and women and charged them with violating Judge

Taylor's injunction that forbade anyone from interfering with the integration process. They were arraigned on December 10 — the same day that Clinton High reopened.

The following month, television's most respected journalist, Edward R. Murrow, broadcast an entire one-hour program on his popular *See It Now* series about Clinton High.

White student Jerry Shattuck, captain of the football team and president of the student council, said on the program, "I didn't ask for integration, and I wasn't enthusiastic about getting it. But the Supreme Court said that our high school should be integrated, and so I thought I should do all I could to bring this court order about peacefully. Our football coach said it very well: 'All through life, you're going to come up against things you don't like, but you're going to have to accept them, anyway, so make the best out of it that you can.' That's the way I feel about it, too, and I think that's the way most of the students feel."

Brittain said on camera that he had previously sided with segregationists until the court ruled otherwise, so he chose to carry out the integration of the school — and had paid the price. "I've suffered nothing but personal harassment as have others, including my wife, teachers, students, and anybody who took a stand to obey the law that they not necessarily agreed with," he said. "Day and night, the phone rings. My life has been threatened ten or twelve times by anonymous callers who hang up. I've had my phone number changed four times. I've had unsigned letters with vile language. One today says someone should throw acid in my face, and that I wasn't fit to live.

"Teachers have been called names of all kinds. These

people [Kasper supporters] have made it difficult for teachers to teach. Most students have behaved loyally. There are forty students who are creating trouble — the youth organization connected with the white citizens' council. Kasper told me that he had two goals: to drive the Negroes out of school and to get me out of my job. If we teach our citizens to disobey this law, they aren't learning the right principles of citizenship. If they can do that, they can violate any other law. It's an amazing thing that in these United States, an American citizen has to be subjected to this while the lawless citizens who don't accept the law continue to run free. I know it's not a true picture of the people of Anderson County."

On the program, JoAnn Allen mentioned that she had made two As, a B, and a C. "My teachers were very proud of me, and my parents were, too, because they thought I did well through all the strain that we went through," she said. "Sometimes I couldn't keep my mind on my lessons because I was thinking about the people [heckling segregationists] on the outside."

Her father, Herbert, who had lived in Clinton for 24 years, announced on camera that he and his family were moving to Los Angeles for a better job for him and a better education for JoAnn. "We aren't leaving here with hatred in our hearts against anyone, even those who are against us," he said. "We do not hate those people because they are misled and they were brought up that way."

The atmosphere at school changed for the better during the second semester. There were no more major incidents for the black students that term — except for one that made them extremely proud. On May 17, 1957, exactly three years to the day of the Supreme Court's *Brown v. Board of Education* decision, Bobby Cain became the first black graduate of an integrated public high school in the Deep South.

An even prouder moment for Theresser was earning her high school diploma three years later. With their diplomas, she and other members of the Clinton 12 had marked their place in history as young foot soldiers in a war that hate couldn't win.

John Kasper was acquitted in a jury trial of all charges in Clinton. However, the following year he was convicted of conspiracy and spent eight months in federal prison. After his release, he continued to fight against school integration throughout the South without success and was often arrested on charges ranging from inciting a riot to disorderly conduct. He finally gave up his battle in 1967 and then spent the rest of his life as a husband and father who held a series of clerical jobs. He died in 1998.

The 1956–57 school term took its toll on the Clinton High staff. Principal Brittain and his wife resigned under the stress of constant harassment and death threats. Brittain, a man with a slight build who typically weighed 130 pounds, lost 14 pounds by the end of the school year. Only seven of the school's teachers chose to stay for the following term.

Theresser's sophomore year was relatively free of racial harassment, and she looked forward to her junior year. But before dawn on October 5, 1958, most of the school was destroyed by three successive blasts from an estimated 100 sticks of dynamite planted by culprits who were never caught. Fortunately, no one was injured.

Residents and volunteers sprang into action. Within a week, they had prepared the unused Linden Elementary School in the nearby town of Oak Ridge, seven miles away, as a replacement high school.

Oak Ridge High and Clinton High were bitter archrivals. But as Theresser and her fellow students stepped off the school buses at their temporary school for the first time, they were greeted by the Oak Ridge High band in full uniform, playing Clinton's school song. For the rest of the year, the displaced students did the best they could to learn while sitting in desks built for much younger children.

Reconstruction of Clinton High was completed in 1960. But it wasn't until 1965 that the all-black Green McAdoo Elementary was finally integrated.

Theresser (who now goes by her first name of Anna) graduated high school and raised a family while working in Oak Ridge in the energy industry for 29 years. She's the mother of three, grandmother of ten, and great-grandmother of five. She seldom spoke about her high school days to her children (who ended up going to Clinton High) until they were adults. Now retired, she occasionally speaks to schools and civic groups about integration.

Today, the Clinton 12 are immortalized with life-size bronze statues in front of the former Green McAdoo school, which has been converted into a cultural center and local civil rights museum.

"The years at Clinton High weren't fun to go through," Anna Theresser Caswell says. "But I'm glad we did it so we could pave the way for future generations."

RODNEY HURST AND AX HANDLE SATURDAY

At first, Rodney Hurst couldn't comprehend what was unfolding in front of him. His fellow demonstrators were running wildly past him down the street . . . and he didn't know why.

Within seconds, the reason for their fleeing became horrifyingly clear to the 16-year-old protest leader: Hundreds of hate-filled white men brandishing ax handles and baseball bats were attacking any black person in their path in downtown Jacksonville, Florida. The die-hard racists were enraged over student-led sit-ins at downtown department-store lunch counters during the previous two weeks — demonstrations aimed at changing a system that had shackled the city's African Americans as second-class citizens.

During the planning stages of the protests, Rodney had pictured in his mind all the possible situations that he thought could occur during the sit-ins. But he never conjured anything remotely close to the savage brutality that was now staining the streets and sidewalks with blood.

There were no policemen anywhere. To stop and help someone who was being beaten with an ax handle meant getting clubbed as well. *All the cops have disappeared!* he thought. *Where are they?*

It was clear to Rodney that everyone was on his own. He began to run — to run for his life.

Growing up in Jacksonville — one of the largest segregated cities in the South — Rodney knew all too well the indignities black people faced on a daily basis, especially in downtown's white-owned department stores. African Americans were not allowed to try on hats, shoes, or clothes out of a warped fear that they somehow would "contaminate" the items for white people. So they had to guess whether or not they were buying the right size. If the item didn't fit, it was their tough luck because they couldn't take it back. These same stores would hire black people only for janitorial jobs and not as clerks or managers.

And there were the constant reminders throughout the city of 373,000 people of how the white community did nothing to curb violent-prone bigots. Two all-white Baptist churches allowed Ku Klux Klan rallies in their parking lots. Rodney often saw members of the KKK — clad in their flowing robes and pointy hats — gather in public parks on Saturday afternoons and spit out their rants of hostility. Not uncommon were shopkeepers, like the barber next door to the Seminole Hotel, where Rodney's stepdad worked as the chief bellman. The barber displayed an ax handle on the wall and called it a "nigger intimidator."

From an early age, Rodney wanted to fight discrimination. He took his first cues from his mother, Janelle "Jan" Saunders Wilson. When no one was looking, she would lift him and his younger sister, Joan, so they could drink out of the whites-only water fountain. One time his mother pointed to the "colored" sign over a water fountain and sarcastically asked the white store manager, "Just what color is it?"

Rodney was 11 when he participated in his first demonstration. In 1955, he joined other African Americans who were carrying signs and walking the picket line outside Sears, Roebuck, a department store that took up a whole city block. They were protesting Sears's discriminatory hiring practices. White onlookers threw firecrackers at the picketers and hurled hurtful insults like, "Niggers, go back to Africa!" and "Jungle bunnies!" For six weeks, black people walked the picket line, but without initial success.

A gifted student, Rodney skipped a grade and attended Isaiah Blocker Junior High, which had no gym, lockers, showers, nor air-conditioning. The cafeteria doubled as the auditorium. Like virtually every black school in the South at the time, Blocker's textbooks, desks, and other equipment were discards from white schools.

But the school had one special asset that no other had — Rutledge Pearson, a tall, dynamic African American who taught history and was always speaking out against racial injustice. On Rodney's first day in his eighth-grade history class, he was surprised when Pearson held up a book and announced to the class, "The textbook for our American History class is *Life in These United States*. It is on the Duval County School Board's list of approved textbooks. Leave it home!" He explained that the textbook — like so many others approved by the segregated school system — ignored African Americans' roles and accomplishments in shaping the country.

Pearson worked his students hard, insisting good wasn't good enough. He had them write letters to famous black people like baseball great Jackie Robinson, tennis and golf legend Althea Gibson, and Judge Thurgood Marshall, who would one day be a Supreme Court justice. Pearson made them participate in panel discussions on current events and assigned them reports that had to be typed, whether the students knew how to use a typewriter or not.

Above all, he encouraged students to join the local Youth Council of the NAACP to work toward racial equality in Jacksonville because, as he often said, "Freedom isn't free. If it's worth having, it's worth making a sacrifice and fighting for it."

Inspired by Pearson's passion for civil rights, Rodney immersed himself in the Youth Council, which was made up mostly of black high school and college students and several young adults. Pearson was their adult advisor.

At the beginning of the 1959–60 school year, Rodney, then a 15-year-old senior at all-black Northwestern Junior-Senior High School, was voted president of the Youth Council, which held meetings at the Laura Street Presbyterian Church.

Motivated by student-led lunch counter sit-ins in other cities, the Youth Council focused its attention on righting a glaring wrong in segregated Jacksonville: "Isn't it strange," Rodney told his fellow members, "that the whites don't mind black people working in their homes but won't let us sit at the lunch counters with them?"

The big downtown department stores — Woolworth's, W. T. Grant, Kress, McCrory's, and Cohen Brothers — insulted black shoppers daily by accepting their money at all the various counters but rejecting their presence at the lunch counter. By far, the biggest downtown lunch counter was at Woolworth's. It seated 84 patrons — whites only, of course. To buy lunch, African Americans had to walk past the jewelry counter, the men's, women's, and children's clothes counters, the "white" and "colored" water fountains, the shoe department, the segregated restrooms, and the house and garden departments before reaching the "colored," windowless 15-seat lunch counter.

So the Youth Council decided to stage a sit-in for equality. "We need to dramatize what the struggle is all about," Rodney told his members. "We want everyone to know that eating a hot dog and drinking a Coke is not our main focus. Our main focus is human dignity and respect."

The Youth Council members were well aware that in many cities, police threw the sit-in demonstrators in jail, where they were beaten under the guise of resisting arrest. Rodney and his fellow students chose "passive resistance" as their tactic for demonstrating. "If provoked, we won't fight back," he told his members. The philosophy mirrored that of Mahatma Gandhi — India's leader for independence through nonviolent civil disobedience — and Dr. Martin Luther King, Jr.

The Youth Council's first sit-in was planned for Saturday, August 13, 1960, targeting the five major downtown department stores. That morning, more than 100 members met at the church, where they prayed and sang freedom songs.

Even though he was only 16 years old, Rodney acted older than his age. He had already graduated from high school, was days away from beginning college, and, as Youth Council president, commanded respect from young and old alike.

In groups of twos and threes, Rodney led them to Woolworth's, arriving at 11 A.M. They purchased items at various counters throughout the store and then occupied the seats at the lunch counter.

A shocked white waitress stared at the black students and declared with a huff, "Coloreds are not served at this lunch counter. Y'all know this is the *white* lunch counter. The *colored* lunch counter is at the back of the store."

The demonstrators didn't move or say anything. Soon James Word, the manager of Woolworth's, showed up and read a prepared statement that said the store reserved the right to deny service to anyone.

"We are here to be served," Rodney told him. "The store accepts our money at all the other counters. It's a contradiction to refuse our money at the lunch counter."

Word then announced, "The lunch counter is closed."

Believing that the store would reopen the counter as soon as they left, the students remained in their seats for another hour. Meanwhile, angry whites began to arrive, shouting insults and racial epithets at the demonstrators.

A middle-aged man wearing a white shirt, tie, and suit leaned on a cane that had been whittled to a fine point. Then, while someone helped him walk, he poked each demonstrator in the back with the cane.

When the sit-in ended and the African Americans started to walk out, white onlookers stuck them with pins and sharp objects, and kicked and shoved them. A white woman stomped her high heel into Rodney's foot as he left the store. He kept walking, refusing to give her the satisfaction of knowing that he was in pain.

One of the main goals of the demonstration was to get media attention for the cause. Rodney couldn't wait to see what had been written in the paper. To his dismay, the city's major newspaper, the *Times-Union*, deliberately ignored Jacksonville's first sit-in, even though it was significant news.

The following Monday and throughout the week, black students continued their sit-ins at the five department stores. And racist whites continued to harass the demonstrators by yelling vile slurs, and elbowing and shoving them. The protestors didn't retaliate; they stuck to their tactic of passive resistance.

Early Saturday morning, August 27, before the next planned sit-in at Woolworth's, Pearson received a troubling phone call about suspicious activities at Hemming Park across the street from the store. Dozens of white men — many in Confederate uniforms — were gathering at the park and carrying ax handles with small Confederate battle flags taped to them. A parked van sported a sign that read FREE AX HANDLES. Pearson and sit-in captain Arnett Girardeau went downtown to see for themselves.

Rodney arrived at the church youth center that morning unaware of the disturbing situation developing eight blocks away. He didn't expect the day's sit-in to be any different than the others. Thirty-four members showed up and sang their usual freedom songs before going over last-minute plans.

Returning from downtown, Pearson and Girardeau told the group what they saw at Hemming Park.

"The Klan was there," Girardeau reported. "They said, 'We're gonna stop these niggers from marching.' I saw ax handles sticking out of the shrubbery. I saw men gathering in Confederate uniforms with more hatred in their eyes than I've ever seen in my life. I fear it's going to be a bad day."

Pearson agreed with the grim assessment. "There likely will be trouble today," he warned. "I tried to call the sheriff to express my concerns, but I couldn't reach him. If any member here doesn't want to participate today, I fully understand."

The members discussed whether or not to go ahead with the sit-in. Some felt that because there was a strong likelihood the KKK would trigger a violent confrontation, the sit-in should be canceled. Others, like Rodney, pressed for the group to stay strong and move forward.

Pearson suggested they pray on it, so the students joined hands. After their prayer, they chanted in unison, "Together we go up, together we stay up."

Before the vote, some members asked Marjorie Meeks — Rodney's friend, classmate, and the Youth Council secretary — what she was going to do. "Nothing will stop me," she answered.

When the same question was posed to Rodney, he declared, "I'm going, no matter what."

The members then took a vote. It was unanimous: The sit-in would go on as planned. Instead of targeting

Woolworth's, however, they decided it would be safer to take over the 30-seat lunch counter at W. T. Grant, three blocks from Hemming Park and away from the gathering mob.

Before marching to Grant's, they sang one of the classic freedom songs:

"*Ain't gonna let nobody turn me 'round,*
Turn me 'round, turn me 'round.
Ain't gonna let nobody turn me 'round.
I'm gonna keep on a-walkin', keep on a-talkin',
Walkin' into freedom land."

With little trouble, they marched down to Grant's and occupied the lunch counter. As expected, the bigots in the store verbally hassled them until store officials closed the lunch counter and turned out the lights in that section of the store.

Rodney was one of the last protestors to leave. When he stepped outside on that steamy, hot day, he entered into the city's worst nightmare. At first, he couldn't figure out what was happening. The demonstrators in front of him had turned around and were running the other way in the street. "What's wrong? What's wrong?" he shouted.

No one answered. Some screamed. His instincts told him to run, too, but from what? He stopped and gazed up Adams Street. What he saw stunned him. A block away, a mob of white men and teens — two hundred, maybe three hundred — were rushing down the street, brandishing baseball bats and ax handles and swinging them at every black person they encountered. It didn't matter if the victims were young demonstrators or Saturday shoppers or elderly strollers or even innocent children. If they were black, they were targeted for a bludgeoning.

By now, black people were fleeing in all directions. And the white attackers were right on their heels. Rodney saw a woman and her young son get slammed to the ground by one of the assailants. *Thank goodness, he didn't hit them with his ax handle*, Rodney thought.

Cars pulled off the street and screeched to a stop. If the driver was black, his vehicle got bashed by bats and ax handles, and his windshield and windows got shattered.

Rodney saw a white cameraman from the local TV station standing on top of a car shooting film of the rampage. A moment later, a man with an ax handle whacked the cameraman behind his legs, causing him to buckle and fall off the vehicle. *They don't want anyone to see footage of this vicious attack*, Rodney thought. *They don't want the world to see the truth.*

Some African Americans, unable to run because of their age or physical condition, sought refuge in stores. Lucky ones slipped inside before employees locked the doors. Unlucky ones who were a moment too late rattled doors that wouldn't open and found themselves easy prey for the ax-brandishing mob.

With no police in sight, Rodney realized he had to flee. He sprinted to Main Street, away from the frenzy, then headed north, praying no attackers would leap out from a side street or alley. He kept running until a car pulled up beside him. The driver was a black woman who attended his church. "Get in!" she yelled. He jumped into the car and they sped off.

"Thank you," said Rodney, trying to catch his breath. "You're a lifesaver." Looking behind him, he told her, "I can't believe this is happening. Our people are getting battered for no reason other than the color of our skin. How is it possible to have that much hate?"

She had no answer. After dropping him off at the Laura Street Presbyterian Church's Youth Center, she told Rodney, "I'm going back to see if I can find others who need a ride."

One by one, the shaken members of the Youth Council made their way back to the church. Some were disoriented, confused, and scared. Some were crying. All were angry. Marjorie broke down and wept because she didn't know the fate of those who hadn't shown up yet. "What is going to happen next?" she wondered out loud.

Rev. Wilbert Miller, pastor of the church, and Pearson did their best to calm everyone as worried parents rushed to the church, looking for their children. Despite the bloodshed, not one parent voiced any regret to Rodney about allowing their children to participate in the sit-ins.

Meanwhile, downtown had turned into a chaotic, bloody melee. Learning of the unprovoked attack, the Boomerangs — a group of black teenagers who lived in the nearby public housing project and didn't believe in passive resistance — charged into the riot to protect the innocent. The Boomerangs' form of protection was to attack the white assailants by wrestling the ax handles away from them and using the weapons to beat them.

Only then did the police arrive and begin to restore some sense of order by making arrests of whites and blacks — mostly blacks.

"When whites attacked blacks, where were the cops?" Rodney fumed. "They had disappeared. But when the

Boomerangs ran downtown to protect their brothers and sisters, the cops and sheriff's deputies were everywhere."

Although relative calm had returned to central downtown, violence flared up in various nearby sections of the city. As whites drove down Ashley Street — the commercial hub of the black community — the pent-up emotions of many residents exploded, and they began hurling rocks. Police quickly arrived and sealed the area, ordering everyone off the street. Those who didn't move fast enough were arrested. Within hours, the street was quiet and in lockdown mode with police patrolling the area.

Late in the afternoon, Rev. J. S. Johnson gathered everyone in the youth center for a prayer. "God is still in charge and won't let anyone turn us around," he told them. "God took us to the hills and the valleys. The die is cast. We will not back down."

As the group sang "We Shall Overcome," tears trickled down Rodney's cheeks. It was the first time all day that he released the terrible sadness in his heart. When he left the church for home, he could feel the air was still fraught with tension.

That night a pickup truck carrying a group of well-armed Klansmen drove into the all-black Blodgett Homes public housing project and began shooting into buildings. Residents returned fire until the truck sped away.

The next morning, the *Times-Union* downplayed the violence, putting the story on page 15 with the headline "Tight Security Lid Is Clamped on City after Racial Strife." It said that "33 Negroes and 9 white persons were arrested on charges ranging from inciting to riot to fighting."

Despite the effort by the paper to stymie the truth, reporters from other newspapers filed stories describing the shocking attack that became national news for several days. No one knew — or would ever know — exactly how many people were arrested or injured. Some media sources said as many as 150 were arrested and 70 were hurt. The number of ax-wielding thugs was estimated at between 100 and 300, many from surrounding towns and from various KKK chapters.

To keep the black community informed, the Youth Council called a mass meeting of students and adults for Sunday evening at St. Paul AME Church. Rodney had planned on reading resolutions calling for a boycott of all downtown department stores and the continuation of the sit-ins.

However, Sol Silverman, of the US Civil Rights Commission, asked the Youth Council to postpone any sit-ins or boycotts and agree to a cooling-off period. He said he wanted time for the commission to investigate the actions of law enforcement and for black leaders and white leaders to begin an honest dialogue. Reluctantly, the Youth Council voted to discontinue the sit-ins, but insisted on going forward with the boycott.

By the start of the mass meeting, Rodney was proud and pleased that the church was jam-packed. The atmosphere inside crackled with emotion and passion over their fight for respect and dignity.

In the first of several resolutions that the Youth Council proposed to the audience, Rodney called upon the US Department of Justice to investigate not only the vicious assaults but also "the failure of law enforcement officers of

Jacksonville and Duval County to provide adequate protection for law-abiding citizens who were attacked by the mob which assembled with bats, ax handles, and clubs [often] in full view of law enforcement officers."

Another resolution asked for the formation of a biracial commission to seek ways to resolve integration issues. After Rodney finished reading the resolutions, the crowd erupted in thunderous applause and choruses of "Amen!"

Jacksonville's mayor, Haydon Burns, an avowed segregationist, wanted nothing to do with a local biracial committee, claiming one wasn't needed. He especially didn't want to deal with the Youth Council leaders.

Before starting fall classes at Jacksonville's predominantly black Edward Waters College, Rodney and Marjorie learned that Mayor Burns had tried to pressure the school's president, William Stewart, into denying admission to the two young activists, who had been awarded scholarships. Burns had warned Stewart that the city's and county's annual donation of $75,000 to the college would be in jeopardy if Rodney and Marjorie attended class there. Stewart brought the issue to the entire faculty and asked the teachers to vote. They overwhelmingly voted to accept the two students' applications. "I would not have rejected your application, but I wanted the faculty apprised of the situation and the threat," Stewart told Rodney.

The Youth Council continued its boycott and resumed picketing, sit-ins, and demonstrations downtown. When Rodney wasn't attending classes, he was involved in protests or speaking throughout the southeast about the struggle for racial equality in Jacksonville.

If Rodney needed any further proof that the mayor was out to get him, it arrived on December 8 when police came onto the campus and arrested him. Juvenile Court Judge Marion Gooding had issued a decree that sit-ins were violent and dangerous activities even though the Youth Council members never assaulted or threatened anyone. The police took Rodney to the juvenile shelter, where he was charged with "contributing to the delinquency of a minor," and then released him to the custody of his mother. The police had earlier arrested a 13-year-old protestor and coerced him into claiming that Rodney had made him protest.

On the day of the hearing, December 12, the boy couldn't point out Rodney in the courtroom. That's because the boy had never met Rodney before. The miffed judge had no choice but to dismiss the case.

After seven months of negotiations, sit-ins, protests, and an effective boycott, the downtown businesses finally agreed to integrate the lunch counters in spring 1961.

The plan called for two black people to eat at Woolworth's white lunch counter for one week, so whites could get used to the idea of having African Americans sitting next to them. The following week, all downtown lunch counters would be open to anyone regardless of race.

"I knew this day would come," Rodney told his fellow members. "I had faith in God."

The next Monday, Rodney and Marjorie sat down at Woolworth's lunch counter and were served by a white waitress. They each had a hamburger and a vanilla milk shake. They didn't toast each other because they knew there was still so much more that needed to be done to achieve racial equality. Nevertheless, the two enjoyed their burgers and shakes because of what the food represented — a small taste of freedom.

Rodney Hurst left college and joined the air force. After his honorable discharge, he became the first black male hired by the Prudential South Center Home Office in Jacksonville. He then worked in public television, becoming the city's first African American to cohost a TV talk show there. He later served two four-year terms on the Jacksonville City Council.

Hurst, who now speaks extensively about racism and civil rights, is the author of It Was Never about a Hot Dog and a Coke!: A Personal Account of the 1960 Sit-in Demonstrations in Jacksonville, Florida, *and* Ax Handle Saturday.

He and his wife, Ann, have two sons and two granddaughters.

Marjorie Meeks Brown, the mother of five and grand-mother of seven, made history as the first female postmaster of Atlanta, Georgia, and was an executive with the United States Postal Service for more than 30 years.

Rutledge Pearson was eventually forced out of the Duval County school system and became an organizer for the International Laundry Workers Union. The respected activist died in a car accident in May 1967 and became the first black person buried in previously segregated Evergreen Cemetery in Jacksonville. An elementary school in Duval County bears his name. After Hurst's first election to the city council in 1975, one of his first accomplishments was getting a bridge named after Pearson.

CHARLEY PERSON AND THE FREEDOM RIDERS

Charley Person was terrified.

It wasn't from the punches to the jaw or the kicks to the gut or even the blow to the head from an iron pipe at the blood-splattered hands of a horde of Ku Klux Klansmen and their supporters.

And it wasn't from worrying if he would be beaten to death because, as a teenage civil rights activist trained in the art of nonviolent resistance, he had been taught *not* to defend himself or fight back.

No, what scared the black student the most as he endured the body blows was seeing the same expression on the contorted faces of each of his white tormentors: Hate. Pure hate.

Up until this day, Charley had never seen such loathing, malice, and hostility directed at anyone. Now all of that was directed at him, someone the assailants had never laid eyes on before. And it frightened him.

How is it possible, he wondered as the pummeling continued, *that they can get so worked up and so full of hate over a complete stranger?*

The answer was simple: Charley was in the Deep South . . . and he was a Freedom Rider.

Less than a year earlier, the career path he had dreamed about became sidetracked by his desire to help end segregation. Charley — whose boyhood friends had nicknamed the Mad Scientist — had wanted to attend Georgia Tech and become a nuclear physicist. He earned the grades to get into Tech, but he didn't have the connections or the right color skin. At the time, the school required applicants to get two recommendations from its all-white alumni — an almost impossible task for a black kid. So he enrolled in the predominantly black Morehouse College in Atlanta in fall 1960.

Inspired by the 1960 sit-ins in Greensboro, North Carolina, the freshman became dedicated to the civil rights movement. He was on the front lines of marches, demonstrations, pickets, and Atlanta's first sit-ins in protest of segregated lunch counters and the lack of jobs for black people in the city's major stores.

During sit-ins, Charley — who would dress up in a shirt and tie and sport coat — used his time sitting at the lunch counters to study while he waited for service that never came. He ignored the angry whites who showered him and his comrades with racial slurs and threats — including one from the guy holding a meat cleaver.

In February 1961, Charley was one of more than 70 college students arrested during a demonstration at

Sprayberry's Cafeteria. At the county jail, the students sang freedom songs and often changed the lyrics to pass information — like how many demonstrators were behind bars — to new arrivals. But Charley was too enthusiastic and too loud, so the jailers wanted to make an example out of him and put him in solitary confinement. For the next five days, he was kept in a windowless eight-foot-by-ten-foot cell lit by a single 40-watt bulb. He was not allowed any books or paper and pencils, so he spent those long, boring hours recalling passages from his philosophy textbooks. He also did a lot of thinking and decided he would become even more committed to the movement after serving his 16-day jail sentence.

A few months later, Charley volunteered for a dangerous mission and was accepted. CORE wanted to test a 1960 Supreme Court decision that segregation was unconstitutional in facilities provided for interstate travelers, such as restaurants, waiting rooms, and restrooms in bus and train terminals. Because most of the Southern states ignored the ruling, CORE decided to confront this blatant contempt for federal law by launching Freedom Rides.

For its initial attempt, CORE selected 13 people — 7 African Americans, including Charley, and 6 white civil rights activists — to ride on regularly scheduled Greyhound and Trailways buses from Washington, DC, to New Orleans. (Five other Riders would join them, some as replacements, along the way.) Stopping at bus stations at various points on the trip, the Riders planned to defy the Jim Crow laws and customs in the Deep South's transit system. They intended to eat together at terminal restaurants and for African Americans to use the whites-only bathrooms and vice versa.

Although it meant that Charley would miss nearly two weeks of classes, he felt this risky operation was worth it. So he traveled to Washington, where he joined the others in intense training in nonviolent, passive resistance. Trying to anticipate what white supremacists might do to them, they swore, spit, and poured drinks on one another and knocked one another to the floor during training sessions.

Realizing that three days of extreme role-playing had emotionally drained everyone in the group, James Farmer, CORE's founder and national director, took the Riders for dinner at a Chinese restaurant. For some, it was the first time they had ever tasted Asian food. During the meal, someone joked, "Eat well because it could be our Last Supper."

On May 4, 1961, the Riders set out on the first leg of their trip on two separate buses and hoped to reach New Orleans on May 17. That date held significance because it would be the seventh anniversary of the Supreme Court's *Brown v. Board of Education* ruling that segregated public schools were unconstitutional.

As his bus pulled out of the terminal, Charley, who at age 18 was the youngest of the Freedom Riders, was pumped with the excitement of knowing he was embarking on a momentous journey. Any worries he harbored that their lives were in jeopardy were buried by an optimistic feeling that the first Freedom Ride would deliver a resounding wallop to Southern segregation.

His confidence remained strong as the group traveled through Virginia and into North Carolina without any hassles over black people using what had been whites-only waiting rooms and restrooms and being served at lunch counters that previously had banned nonwhites.

But Charley got a bitter lesson in reality after the bus pulled into the station in Charlotte. He hopped onto a whites-only shoe-shine chair and asked to have his shoes polished. When he was refused service, Charley remained seated, claiming he wouldn't leave until the policy against black customers was changed. When a police officer threatened to arrest him, however, Charley left. Joe Perkins, 27, a black CORE field secretary, then tried to get his shoes shined there and promptly became the first Freedom Rider to get arrested on the trip.

At the next stop, Rock Hill, South Carolina, John Lewis, a 21-year-old black seminary student and member of SNCC, walked into the whites-only bus terminal bathroom. Seconds later, he was assaulted by a gang of racist whites. As they punched and kicked Lewis, fellow Rider Albert Bigelow, a white 55-year-old navy veteran, tried to stand between him and the brutes. With his hands by his side and unwilling to defend himself, Bigelow was beaten up, too. A cop who had watched the attack the whole time finally told the hoodlums to "get on home." Although Lewis was bleeding from several facial cuts and was suffering bruised ribs, he refused medical attention.

When the bus arrived in Chester, South Carolina, local officials ordered the doors to the bus station locked. In Winnsboro, two Riders were arrested. Henry "Hank" Thomas, a 19-year-old Howard University student, was hauled off after he sat down at the terminal's whites-only counter. When Jim Peck, 46, a white CORE member, got involved, he was also taken to jail. The two were soon released and rejoined the group the next day.

Reaching Atlanta, Georgia, on May 13, the Riders had dinner with Dr. Martin Luther King, Jr., who praised their courage and dedication. Everyone was in high spirits until late at night when word reached them that the KKK was planning to meet them in Birmingham, Alabama. Because that meant probable harm to the Riders, they were given the chance to back out, but none did. Charley told himself, *What's the worst that could happen? We get a little roughed up. I can deal with that.*

At noon the following day — an hour after seven Freedom Riders had left on a Greyhound bus — the rest of the group climbed aboard a Birmingham-bound Trailways bus and settled in for the scheduled four-hour trip. Charley sat in the front seat next to Herman Harris, a black 21-year-old Morris College student. Farther in the back were Jim Peck; Ivor "Jerry" Moore, a black 21-year-old Morris College student; and Isaac "Ike" Reynolds, 27, a black CORE field secretary. The other Riders were husband and wife Walter and Frances Bergman, ages 61 and 57 respectively. The two were retired educators from Michigan who had "adopted" Charley and bonded with him. Seated in the rear were two black journalists from the magazine *Jet*, reporter Simeon Booker and photographer Ted Gaffney, who were documenting the trip.

Charley noticed that among the passengers who got on the bus in Atlanta were several rough-looking, burly white men in their late twenties. One of them was wearing bib overalls and a long-sleeved red plaid shirt. Charley thought that was strange because it was a warm, sunny day.

When the bus reached the open road, the tough guys made it clear they were white supremacists. Addressing Charley and the other African Americans on board, one of the men declared, "You niggers will be taken care of once you get in Alabama." Another one told the white activists, "You nigger lovers are a disgrace to the white race."

The Riders began to worry that their reception in Alabama would be much more troubling and perilous than what they had experienced so far.

After traveling for two hours, the bus made a brief rest stop in Heflin, about 15 miles inside the Alabama state line. The man in the bib overalls and red shirt stood up and told Charley in a threatening voice for all to hear, "You niggers have had it good in Georgia, but you're in Alabama now." Then he got off.

What's he know that we don't? Charley wondered. He could feel the nervous tension tighten his body.

About a half hour later, the bus pulled into the Anniston Trailways station, where Peck and Walter Bergman bought sandwiches for their group. The driver, who had stepped off to talk to a couple of police officers, returned with eight Klansmen behind him. "We have received word that a Greyhound bus has been burned to the ground and passengers are being carried to the hospital by the carloads," the driver announced.

Some of the Riders gasped. The news shocked Charley. *Is he lying to us? Is he trying to scare us? Could there be that much hate against us Negroes that they would torch a bus?*

"A mob is waiting for our bus," the driver continued. "And they'll do the same to us unless we get these niggers off the front seats," he added, pointing to Charley and Herman.

"Sir, you realize that we are all interstate passengers who, according to the laws of the land, have the right to sit wherever we please," Peck told him.

The driver shook his head in disgust and walked out.

One of the Klansmen stepped forward and bellowed to Charley and Herman, who remained in the front seats, "Niggers get back! You ain't up North. You're in Alabama, and niggers ain't worth nothin' here."

Then he lunged toward Charley and sucker-punched him in the face. The blow momentarily stunned Charley, but he didn't feel any real pain. The 5-foot-6, 136-pound student got hit again and again. But following the principles that he had been taught, he didn't fight back or block punches or even cover up. *Just take their best shot,* he told himself.

The same was true for Herman, who was attacked by another Klansman. The defenseless students were then dragged into the aisle, where they were pummeled and kicked repeatedly.

Pleading with the attackers to stop, Peck and Walter Bergman rushed toward the front. One of the brutes struck Peck so hard that the short, skinny activist sailed across two rows of seats. When Bergman, who was the oldest in the group, reached the front, he was socked in the jaw and sent crashing to the floor.

Incensed that whites would even think of coming to the aid of black people, the attackers continued to work over Peck and Bergman while shouting, "This is what happens to nigger lovers in Alabama!" While one Klansman held up

Peck's bloodied head, others kept hitting him in the face until he passed out. Bergman too was so beat up that he lost consciousness, but that didn't stop one assailant from stomping on his chest.

Screaming in horror, Frances begged the attacker, "Stop! Stop! You're killing my husband!"

Without looking up, the Klansman continued his assault, telling Frances, "Shut up, you nigger lover!" He stopped only after he was ordered to by another KKK thug. Peck and Bergman were then picked up and dumped on the backseat. Barely conscious, Charley and Herman were also lugged to the back and stacked on top of the two white men, creating a bloody pile of victims.

The savagery that Frances witnessed sent her into tears. "How could you beat up innocent unarmed men and students?" she wailed.

Pleased with the brutality they had inflicted, the Klansmen took seats in the middle of the bus to prevent any of the four black students from trying to sit in the front. "Ain't nobody but whites sittin' up here!" declared a Klansman. "And them nigger lovers can just sit back there with their nigger friends."

A few minutes later, the driver returned to the bus with a police officer. Seeing the blood on the floor and the battered activists groaning in the back, the cop grinned and told the assailants, "Don't worry 'bout no lawsuits, boys. I ain't seen a thing." As he left, he motioned for the bus to leave.

At the officer's suggestion, the driver took a different route than normal to avoid the waiting mob ahead. On the 90-minute ride to Birmingham, the Klansmen continued to taunt the Freedom Riders and threaten them by displaying a pistol and a steel pipe. "Wait 'til you see the welcome y'all gonna get in Birmin'ham," one of them said. "Yessirree," added another. "Y'all gonna get what's comin' to ya."

Bruised and hurting, Charley and Herman were concerned about the physical condition of Peck and Bergman, who both had regained consciousness. Peck's face and much of his clothes were covered in blood. Bergman was moaning from the pain and found it difficult to sit up.

Charley and Peck had been chosen earlier in the day to test the facilities at the Trailways depot in Birmingham, a city where the Ku Klux Klan and the police were bosom buddies. When the bus arrived at the station at 4:15 P.M., Peck, who could barely stand, asked Charley, "Are you sure you want to do this?"

"Yes, but are you in any shape to go with me?" When Peck nodded, Charley said, "Then let's go."

After the Klansmen got off to join a small gathering of white men in front of the terminal, the Freedom Riders exited the bus to retrieve their luggage. Meanwhile, Charley and Peck cautiously walked toward the whites-only waiting room. The plan called for Charley to go into the white bathroom and Peck in the colored one and then meet at the lunch counter, where they would order something to eat.

As they headed to the door of the station, Charley didn't see any weapons on the whites, who were milling around outside. In fact, he found it odd that they were rather quiet and not making any threatening gestures at him.

But once inside, Charley and Peck found themselves quickly surrounded by angry white men. Pointing to the blood caked on Peck's face and clothes, someone shouted, "That nigger attacked that white man! He deserves to die!"

Charley took a deep breath, resigned over what he was about to face. *I'm going to get a beating.*

"No! No!" Peck yelled in protest. "He didn't attack me. We were both beaten up on the bus by Klansmen!"

"Get the nigger!" a voice rang out.

Charley got pushed toward the colored waiting room, but he managed to spin free and was making his way toward the lunch counter when he was shoved hard against a concrete wall. Suddenly, a flurry of fists slammed into his head. Propped up against the wall, he felt his knees go weak.

Rushing to help him, Peck declared to the attackers, "You'll have to kill me before you hurt him!"

Several hefty men then punched Peck, who went down in a bloody heap. They grabbed him and Charley and pushed the two into a dimly lit corridor where about a dozen whites, some armed with lead pipes, were waiting. In an instant, they were pounding the two Freedom Riders who, once again, refused to fight back.

While he was getting battered, Charley felt a wave of fright from the looks of sheer hatred spread on the faces of his attackers. As his mind processed the terrible images, he was clubbed in the back of the head by someone gripping a pipe. Stunned by the blow, Charley could feel the blood seeping down the back of his neck. He was in such shock that he could barely feel the punches or kicks anymore as he waited for another strike to the head.

But then the flash of a camera caused the assailants to stop. They turned around and when they realized that a photographer had taken a picture of the attack, they went after him. They seized his camera and smashed it and then beat him up.

While their attention was focused on the photographer, Charley got to his feet and staggered out into the street. As luck would have it, a city bus stopped for him. He got on and rode a few blocks.

At a pay phone, he called Rev. Fred Shuttlesworth, a black civil rights leader in Birmingham, who then dispatched someone to pick him up. Charley was taken to three black doctors but none would treat him because they were afraid the state would take away their license to practice for helping a "rabble-rouser" or "outsider," as local white officials termed the Freedom Riders. Finally, a nurse at Rev. Shuttlesworth's Bethel Baptist Church treated Charley and put a special bandage on his head.

Eventually, the rest of the group from the Trailways bus and the Greyhound bus made their way to the church. When Peck, who had been battered into unconsciousness at the station, showed up, he was taken to the hospital, where he received 53 stitches.

At a mass meeting that evening, the Riders shared their harrowing experiences with the audience. Walter Bergman said that when he went into the station's waiting room, he had been knocked to the ground, but he crawled to safety on his hands and knees. His wife, Frances, said she escaped by getting on a passing city bus. Ike Reynolds told the group he had been kicked and punched and tossed into a garbage bin. Jerry Moore and Herman Harris reported that they managed to slip away undetected by the mob. The black journalists, Simeon Booker and Ted Gaffney, said they found a black cabdriver who agreed to spirit them off.

They soon learned that the Birmingham police had agreed to stay away from the bus station for 15 minutes to give the Klansmen free rein to attack the Freedom Riders. By the time the police finally arrived, the assailants were long gone.

But even more appalling to Charley and his Trailways companions was hearing the horror stories of mayhem and near death told by their comrades from the burned-out Greyhound.

The Riders in that bus were their leader Joe Perkins; Albert Bigelow; Hank Thomas; Genevieve Hughes, a 28-year-old white CORE field worker; Jimmy McDonald, a 29-year-old black folk singer and CORE volunteer; Mae Frances Moultrie, a 24-year-old black Morris College student; and Ed Blankenheim, a 27-year-old white carpenter from Arizona. They had left on the Greyhound an hour ahead of the Trailways group. As their bus approached Anniston, Alabama — a town known for its violent Klansmen — a white man stopped it and warned the driver that an unruly crowd was waiting for the Freedom Riders.

Moments after the bus arrived at the station, it was surrounded by a shouting mob of about 50 white men carrying metal pipes, bats, and chains. "Well, boys, here they are," the driver told them. "I brought you some niggers and nigger lovers."

The scared passengers locked the door and closed the windows. The incensed horde slashed tires and smashed windows with rocks and brass knuckles. By the time the

Anniston police showed up, the bashed bus looked like it had been in a bad traffic accident. After some friendly chatter with people in the crowd, the cops escorted the crippled Greyhound out of town. The bus was followed by about three dozen cars and pickups filled with white racists and even families who had come from church. At the city limits, the cops turned back, leaving the bus unprotected.

Six miles outside of town, the flat tires forced the driver to pull over to the side of the road in front of a family-run grocery store on a remote stretch of Highway 202. While the driver went into the store to call someone who could replace the tires, the onrushing bigots swarmed around the bus and began shattering more windows with bats and crowbars. Having again locked themselves inside, the passengers could do nothing but cower.

Two highway patrolmen came on the scene but made no effort to disperse the crowd. Someone then tossed a flaming bundle of gas-soaked rags through a broken window, sending dark gray smoke throughout the bus. Yelling, "Burn them alive!" and "Fry the niggers and their nigger lovers!" several members of the mob leaned against the door to keep the passengers from opening it.

The smoke grew blacker as the flames ignited the upholstered seats. Crouching down in the middle of the bus, Genevieve Hughes screamed, "Oh my God, they're going to burn us up!"

She crawled toward the front, spotted a busted window, squeezed through it, and dropped to the ground. Just then the fuel tank exploded. The hatemongers who were keeping the door closed retreated, worried the whole bus would blow to smithereens. This allowed the rest of the choking, gagging passengers to open the door and escape the flames.

When Hank Thomas crawled away from the bus, a white man went up to him and asked, "Are y'all okay?" Before Thomas could answer, the man struck him in the head with a baseball bat. Thomas fell to the ground, barely conscious.

Onlookers in front of the grocery store stood and watched. Only a few offered to help the victims. One of them was 12-year-old Janie Miller, who ran back and forth, giving the suffering passengers glasses of water as Klansmen cussed her for helping the Riders. (For this act of kindness, she and her family were run out of town by the KKK.)

When state troopers fired a few warning shots in the air, the white supremacists backed away from the dazed Riders, who were sprawled on the grass a few yards from the burning bus. Eventually, the attackers left without the police questioning any of them.

Besides being cut and bruised, several Riders had inhaled smoke and fumes and needed medical attention. After the white victims were loaded into an ambulance, the driver refused to take the African Americans. Insisting that they wouldn't leave their black comrades behind, the white Riders began to get out of the ambulance. Finally, the driver agreed to take everyone and drove them to Anniston Memorial Hospital.

Several Klansmen tried but failed to block the ambulance from getting to the emergency room. Later, while the Riders were being treated, a menacing crowd gathered outside and threatened to burn down the building. Panicky hospital officials ordered the Riders to leave immediately. But they couldn't because the police refused to transport or even escort them out of town.

Joe Perkins called Fred Shuttlesworth in Birmingham. Knowing that the Riders were in serious danger, the pastor mobilized a fleet of eight cars that raced to Anniston and picked them up as police held back the jeering crowd.

Now at the Bethel Baptist Church meeting, all the Riders except Peck, who was still in the hospital in Birmingham, reaffirmed their desire to continue the trip. Even though some of the Riders were still feeling the effects of smoke inhalation and others like Walter Bergman were nursing cracked ribs, they each took turns speaking to the audience.

Charley, whose luggage and jacket were stolen off the bus, was weak and groggy. But he got up and told the people he was grateful they were there. "We are hurting," he said, pointing to the bandage on his head. "We are war-weary from the attacks. I just can't understand how those white people could be so vicious toward us. But we are not deterred and even though we don't know what danger is ahead of us, we must continue the Freedom Rides. We are determined."

Throughout the meeting, the church rocked with shouts of "Amen!" Freedom songs belted out from the heart left everyone in tears. For Charley, it was the most emotional night of his young life.

Rev. Shuttlesworth capped off the evening with a brief sermon in which he said, "It was a wonderful thing to see these young students — Negro and white — come here, even after the mobs and the bus burning. When white and black men are willing to be beaten up together, it is a sure sign they will soon walk together as brothers."

*   *   *

Because of the danger, no driver for Trailways or Greyhound was willing to take the wheel of a bus if Charley and the other Freedom Riders were on board. And no law enforcement agency in Alabama was willing to protect them. So with the help of US Attorney General Robert Kennedy's office, they were put on a flight to New Orleans to complete the trip.

Fearing that violence would only intensify against further Freedom Rides, CORE suspended them. But members of the Nashville Student Movement and SNCC immediately stepped up to continue the Rides. Explained Fisk University student Diane Nash, one of the founders of SNCC, "We cannot let violence overcome nonviolence."

Within days after the original Freedom Ride ended short of its goal, new Riders from Tennessee headed to Montgomery, Alabama, where they were badly beaten by hundreds of hate-mongers. Federal troops had to be called out to protect Riders and 1,500 supporters in that city.

The brutality the Riders encountered had an opposite effect than what the bigoted perpetrators had intended. The struggles faced by the Riders triggered nationwide publicity, outrage, and sympathy. Rather than intimidate, the violent reaction of white supremacists inspired fair-minded people to take up the cause for civil rights. Throughout the summer, hundreds of Americans, black and white, from all over the country, volunteered to travel on Freedom Rides.

When Riders arrived in Jackson, Mississippi, they were arrested, convicted, and sentenced to hard time in Parchman State Penal Farm, notorious for its harsh treatment of prisoners. But for every Rider who was arrested, someone else — a student, a retiree, a white, a black — headed on a Freedom Ride into the Deep South. In Jackson alone, more than 300 Riders were arrested and shipped to Parchman. And still they came.

By the end of summer 1961, about 1,000 people had participated in Freedom Rides, many of them more than once. Their efforts finally led to a crackdown by the Interstate Commerce Commission to enforce the law ending segregation in interstate travel.

Returning home following the original Freedom Ride, Charley Person joined the United States Marines and served for 20 years, including a tour of duty in the Vietnam War. He eventually settled in Atlanta and became an electronics technician for Atlanta Public Schools until his retirement in 2007. Disabled by the effects of Agent Orange — a chemical used to destroy jungle vegetation in Vietnam — Person continues to do community work. He is married with five adult children.

As of 2014, Person is one of only three surviving members of the original 13 Freedom Riders. The other two are John Lewis, now a well-known congressman and civil rights leader, and Hank Thomas, a successful Atlanta businessman and civic leader.

"Don't ever give up doing what you know is right," Person says. "One person can make a difference, and if you're passionate about an issue, you'll find there are like-minded individuals who support your ideas. That's how movements like the Freedom Rides get started."

HENRY STEELE AND THE "JAIL NO BAIL" PROTESTORS

Sixteen-year-old Henry Steele lay exhausted on a paper-thin mat on the cold, dank floor of the Leon County Jail. His muscles ached from digging ditches on an inmate road gang that was hounded all day by an ornery, shotgun-waving guard who kept yelling, "Work harder, harder!" Henry's stomach gurgled from the disgusting, unrecognizable slop that he had been fed that morning and later that evening.

Trying to get comfortable on a wooden pallet that acted as his cot because all the beds were taken, Henry pulled the smelly, ratty blanket over his tall, slender frame. He thought about his parents, who had been standing outside the jail when he and the other inmates had trudged back from their work detail earlier in the evening. His mother had cried as he walked by her, and now he wondered if her tears flowed because she thought he looked so pitiful in his ill-fitting, jail-issued blue overalls or that she worried he would miss too much school while he served out his sentence.

Henry didn't have to be in jail. He *chose* to be there.

He could have been free by having his parents post a bond and file an appeal. Or he simply could have paid the $300 fine that the judge had imposed on him and each of ten black demonstrators after they were found guilty of various charges stemming from the first full-scale lunch counter sit-in in Tallahassee, Florida.

But the high school boy and seven students at Florida A&M University (FAMU) wanted to serve out their 60-day sentences as a form of protest against racial discrimination. They had taken the words of Dr. Martin Luther King, Jr., to heart: "We've got to fill the jails in order to win our equal rights."

Resorting to an untried tactic that confounded their enemies and inspired their supporters in the civil rights movement, Henry and his fellow prisoners were the first students in the country to follow a moral principle known as "jail no bail." In fact, Henry was the first high school student to do it.

Nonviolent civil disobedience was in Henry's blood. His father, Rev. C. K. Steele, was a respected civil rights activist and pastor of Tallahassee's Bethel Missionary Baptist Church. Rev. Steele along with Dr. King and several other clergymen had formed the famed Southern Christian Leadership Council (SCLC), a group devoted to promoting nonviolent social change and ending segregation in the South. He was the organization's first vice president.

Henry grew up in Florida's segregated capital city, where about a third of the residents were African Americans who worked at low-paying jobs, lived in all-black neighborhoods, and attended all-black schools. It was in this environment that Henry's father preached that the most powerful way to change life for the better was through peaceful direct action.

When Henry was 13, he saw firsthand the effectiveness of nonviolence — but also its violent consequences. On May 26, 1956, Wilhelmina Jakes and Carrie Patterson, students at historically black FAMU, got on a crowded city bus, paid their 10-cent fare, and sat down in the only seats available, which were in the whites-only section. When they refused the driver's demand to move to the back of the bus, he ordered them off. They asked for their money back, but he wouldn't give it to them and instead had them arrested. Wilhelmina and Carrie were charged with inciting a riot.

Students on campus were outraged and launched a city-wide bus boycott. It was similar to the ongoing boycott in Montgomery, Alabama, that began six months earlier after bus passenger Rosa Parks was arrested for failing to give up her seat to a white woman.

In Tallahassee, Rev. Steele was elected president of the Inter-Civic Council (ICC), a group of local activists charged with running the boycott against the bus company. The protest had less to do with sitting in the front of the bus and more about ending unjust laws, customs, and traditions that were becoming increasingly intolerable to black people.

Because about 80 percent of the riders of city buses were

African American and now needed transportation, the ICC organized car pools that chauffeured them to and from their jobs. Supporters believed the boycott, which crippled the bus company, would lead to a fairly quick resolution. Instead, it led to violence.

The Steele home, where Henry lived with his parents and five siblings, became a target of vicious retaliation. In the middle of the night, thugs would drive by and shoot into the house or hurl rocks and bricks through the windows. During such attacks, Henry and the other children had been taught to huddle in a windowless hallway. One night, Henry's older brother, Charles, was reading in his upstairs bedroom when bullets shattered his window, showering him with shards of glass. The bullet holes over the doorway, in the stairs, and throughout the venetian blinds were daily reminders of the dangers they faced.

Despite the harassment, Henry's father never flinched. One evening Rev. Steele was at a meeting when Ku Klux Klansmen burned a cross in the family's front yard. When he returned home, the slender, bespectacled pastor — his hat cocked to the side and his bow tie slightly crooked — gazed at the charred grass and declared, "I am not afraid."

And neither was Henry. In his mind, the threats, intimidation, and hostility went with the territory in the war against injustice. He was greatly influenced by his father, who always remained calm except when preaching from the pulpit or delivering a speech against racial inequality. At an ICC meeting, Rev. Steele told fellow members, "They have thrown rocks, they have smashed car windows, they have burned crosses. Well, I am happy to state here tonight that I have no fear of them and, praise God, I have no hate for them."

Henry was in awe over how his dad dealt with bigots who regularly made threatening phone calls. Rather than hang up each time, Rev. Steele remained unruffled and tried to engage the racist caller in a conversation. Usually, the caller became so befuddled he hung up on him. But sometimes, Rev. Steele was able to encourage the person into a meaningful conversation.

One time, Henry went into the den to inform his father dinner was ready. Rev. Steele was on the phone, calmly talking about peace and love and Jesus to one of his tormentors who had threatened him. "Excuse me," Steele told the person. "I've been called to supper. If you'll call back in thirty minutes, we can continue our talk." After dinner, the phone rang again. It was the racist.

Although most of the death threats Rev. Steele received were nothing more than weak attempts at scaring him, occasionally a warning was taken seriously. As a precaution during such times, some members of his church stood guard outside Henry's house.

One night, Henry found his father sitting by the front window, looking distressed and holding a loaded Smith & Wesson revolver in his lap. Henry could tell that his dad felt conflicted and was having a difficult time justifying the use of a weapon. As peace-loving as he was, Rev. Steele would do anything necessary to protect his family. Fortunately, he never had to pull the trigger.

Physical danger wasn't the only peril that the family faced. They were hurting financially, especially after Rev.

Steele took on the hefty money burden of the ICC. He and 21 drivers in the ICC car pool during the bus boycott were arrested and charged with illegally operating a transportation system. City Judge John Rudd found all the defendants guilty and levied a fine of $500 against each one. Rev. Steele took it upon himself to pay off the $11,000 in fines. He hit the lecture circuit and traveled up North visiting churches — sometimes as many as five in one Sunday — making speeches and asking for donations. (It would take him five years to earn the money.)

With the car pool dismantled, most African Americans were forced to get to work on foot. "Walk in dignity than ride in humiliation!" Rev. Steele urged them. Thanks to the boycott, which lasted seven months, and a Supreme Court ruling that segregated buses were unconstitutional, Tallahassee's municipal bus system was finally integrated.

So it was only natural that when the opportunity arose in 1960, Henry chose to participate in the region's first sit-in. At ICC meetings, he had met Patricia and Priscilla Stephens, black sisters who attended FAMU and had been trained in nonviolent direct action by CORE.

Henry, who was a junior in high school, and his brother, Charles, a senior, volunteered to join the Stephens sisters and six other FAMU students in a sit-in at Woolworth's lunch counter. On Saturday February 13, Henry, Charles, and the others strode into the store, sat at the lunch counter, and asked for slices of cake.

The stunned waitress told them, "I'm sorry, but I can't serve you." The students didn't leave but quietly remained in their seats, waiting for the cake they knew they wouldn't get. Angered by the audacity of black students to sit at a whites-only lunch counter, white shoppers flocked behind the demonstrators and began shouting insults and racial slurs: "Niggers, get out of here!" "You niggers are stinking up the joint!" "Y'all ain't wanted here!"

For nearly two hours of verbal abuse, Henry and his fellow sit-in comrades stared at the books they had brought, although no one was really reading. Some whites tried to goad Henry and the others into a fight, but the students remained cool and quiet until the store manager closed the counter. Then they left before anyone thought to call the police.

The following Saturday, February 20, 17 African Americans — Henry, Charles, the Stephens sisters, 12 other FAMU students, and a 43-year-old housekeeper named Mary Ola Gaines — walked into Woolworth's and headed for the lunch counter. "Oh, Lord, here they come again!" exclaimed the same waitress. Like before, they ordered slices of cake. And like before, they were denied. So they remained seated and pulled out their books.

A crowd of young white males — their hair slicked back and the collars of their short-sleeved shirts turned up — had gathered behind the black students and began harassing them: "You niggers eat in the back!" "I thought I smelled niggers!"

The African Americans did their best to ignore the taunts, the shoves, the pokes in the back. The longer the demonstrators sat in silence, the madder the whites got. Henry not only felt their wrath, but also a rage that was rising inside him. Then he thought about a line his father often preached: "Where there is any power as strong and as eternal as love using nonviolence, the promise will be ful-filled." Henry calmed himself and remained quiet. He and his comrades stayed put even after the counter was closed.

After about 90 minutes, Mayor Hugh Williams arrived with five police officers. "As mayor of Tallahassee, I am ask-ing you to leave," he told them.

"We don't intend to leave until we're served our cake," said Priscilla, who had been chosen by the others to act as their spokesperson.

The mayor stormed over to her sister, Patricia, pointed to the "closed" sign, and snarled, "Can you read?" Patricia nodded. The mayor again told them to get out.

"If we don't leave, would we be committing a crime?" Priscilla asked.

"You will be arrested," he replied. Six FAMU students who didn't want to see the inside of a jail cell got up and left the store. Henry and the other ten remained. Frustrated, the mayor ordered the police to arrest them.

A smirk spread across Henry's face. *We're being arrested for sitting at a lunch counter and asking for a slice of cake. That's just crazy.*

As the officers marched the eleven protestors the few blocks to the police station, white bystanders applauded the police and jeered the African Americans. Even though Henry had never been arrested, he wasn't scared or ashamed. He held his head high.

After they were fingerprinted and booked at the police station, they were soon bailed out. Two days later, the sit-in demonstrators appeared in court and pleaded not guilty to the charges of "engaging in riotous conduct and assembly to the disturbance of the public tranquillity." The trial was set for March 3. Furious over the arrests, the FAMU student body voted to skip classes so they could attend the trial. When the judge heard that 3,000 students planned to jam the courthouse, he postponed the trial for two weeks.

On March 12, black students from FAMU and white students from Florida State University (FSU) joined forces and held sit-ins at the lunch counters of both Woolworth's and McCrory's department stores. Henry and the others who had been arrested after the first sit-in thought it best not to participate, but they did observe from outside.

In the demonstration, the white students sat at the lunch counter and were served. Then the black students arrived and ordered. When they were denied service, the whites shared their meals with them. Because the mixing of races at a lunch counter violated Southern customs, the police arrested both black and white demonstrators.

With cops on either side of them, the students were escorted to jail in interracial pairs while prejudiced onlookers shouted "Niggers!" and "Nigger lovers!"

To take the place of those arrested, two new groups of white FSU students and black FAMU students showed up at the two department stores. The demonstrators who arrived at McCory's were immediately taken into custody. Those who reached Woolworth's were met by armed thugs from the racist white citizens' council. The hooligans flashed knives and brandished baseball bats, ax handles, and boards with nails sticking out. The hostile bigots blocked the students from entering while the police looked the other way.

The students stood in front of the threatening mob and chanted, "No violence! No violence! No violence!" To avoid further trouble, the students turned around and regrouped at the FAMU campus. There, Patricia and Priscilla organized more than 1,000 students, including Henry, for a march protesting the day's arrests.

Carrying signs such as WE WILL NOT FIGHT MOBS; GIVE US BACK OUR STUDENTS; WE WANT OUR RIGHTS: WE ARE AMERICANS, TOO; and NO VIOLENCE, the students walked two by two toward downtown.

But after only a few blocks, they were stopped by a line of law enforcement officers from the city, county, and state. City Commissioner William Mayo stepped forward and, through his bullhorn, ordered everyone to turn back or face severe consequences. "You have three minutes to disperse," he announced.

Seconds later — before anyone had time to react to his demand — police began lobbing tear gas canisters. Coughing and screaming, students bolted in all directions. Some collapsed from the fumes; others blinded by the gas staggered helplessly about. Several of those who escaped the tear gas attack suffered the misfortune of running into white citizens' council punks who took advantage of the turmoil and assaulted them.

Henry was several rows back and managed to sprint away from the clouds of tear gas. Patricia wasn't so lucky. An officer popped a canister right in front of her, rendering her unable to see or breathe. Someone grabbed Patricia and led her to a nearby church, where she slowly regained her sight and ability to inhale without hacking.

The march that ended in chaos led to six arrests and the hospitalization of several students who were overcome by the tear gas. One of the persons arrested was white FSU student Virginia Delavan, editor of the school newspaper, the *Flambeau*. She was briefly jailed for simply interviewing some of the black marchers.

Shortly before the bench trial for Henry and the other ten persons charged in the sit-in, the defendants discussed what they would do when they were convicted — not if. They knew they would be found guilty because it would be a sham court proceeding. They assumed the judge would impose either a fine or jail time.

"We should not pay a fine to support a system that does not treat us as equal human beings," Patricia told the group. "We should not pay for segregation. I'm fully aware that some of you can't afford to stay in jail and miss school or work. Priscilla and I have decided that if we have to go to jail to further our cause, then we'll go to jail." She said that by doing so, it might help expose Tallahassee's white establishment as hypocritical and morally bankrupt.

Henry said he would be willing to do jail time, too. So would FAMU students John Broxton, his sister Barbara, William Larkins, Angela Nance, and Clement Carney. Charles wanted to join them, but because he was only two months away from graduating high school, he agreed with his parents that he would pay any fine. Mrs. Gaines — who was fired from her housekeeping job for participating in the sit-in — and FAMU student Merritt Spaulding decided they, too, would choose a fine over jail.

Although Henry's mother, Lois, was against him serving time, his father supported his decision. "You and the others are soldiers of the movement," Rev. Steele told him. "Without the students, there will be no movement."

On March 17, the trial began with Judge John Rudd claiming the charges had nothing to do with race. But Henry and the others knew that it was all about race. *How is ordering food at a lunch counter a crime?* he wondered. *It's only a crime because we're Negroes.*

During testimony, white witnesses — especially Mayor Williams — repeatedly referred to the sit-in demonstrators as "niggers." Henry could only bite his tongue and shake his head over the slurs. The manager of Woolworth's testified that he closed the lunch counter not because the demonstrators were black but because their presence "seemed to cause apprehension on the part of some of the people in the store." The mayor testified that he ordered the arrests because the sit-in was "dangerous to the safety and welfare of the community."

To no one's shock, Judge Rudd found all 11 guilty and told them they each faced a $300 fine or 60 days in jail. The judge and others in the courtroom expected all 11 to pay the fine, as was typical of students in similar cases. So when the eight announced they would appeal and do jail time instead of getting out on bail, observers in the room murmured in surprise.

The convicted defendants' decision meant they would become the first sit-in demonstrators in the country to choose to go to jail rather than pay a fine or post bail on appeal. Their act of defiance reverberated throughout the South among civil rights activists, triggering a rallying cry of "Jail no bail!"

Henry wasn't scared when he arrived at the county jail. As a 16-year-old, he thought he was tough and could handle whatever abuse came his way. To him, it was more of an adventure — and a way to skip school. But he became more apprehensive when the jailer told him and the others, "You niggers have been causin' all that trouble in town, but you ain't gonna in here. No, sir. The folks in here don't like troublemakers. Y'all make it bad for everyone else, so they're gonna make it bad for you."

While the females were forced to scrub the floors and walls of the jails, the males were sent out on a road gang to clean out county ditches. The work was tedious and hard, and made worse by a sadistic guard who pushed the inmates to the brink of exhaustion. Henry figured the guard was making it tough on the prisoners so the guard could look good to the sheriff. Fortunately for Henry, the guard went easier on him, apparently because the student was the youngest on the road gang.

That first night, after a stomach-upsetting dinner of greasy fatback and undercooked grits, Henry tried to get some sleep. But the guards kept everyone up by rattling the cell bars with their billy clubs and yelling, "Sweet dreams, niggers!"

The day after the Tallahassee 8 were locked up, Rev. King sent a telegram to Rev. Steele but addressed to the jailed students. It said in part: "You have again proven that there is nothing more majestic and sublime than the courage of individuals willing to suffer and sacrifice for the cause of freedom [. . .] Going to jail for a righteous cause is a badge of honor and a symbol of dignity [. . .]"

On the third day of imprisonment, a Sunday, hundreds of sympathizers — blacks and whites of all ages — gathered outside the jail and sang inspiring songs and hymns loud enough for the prisoners to hear.

To check on the condition of the students, Rev. Steele and Rev. Daniel Speed visited the jail every day, often bringing them notes of encouragement from home. The clergymen also smuggled letters out — mostly written by Patricia Stephens and Barbara Broxton — that were printed in various publications.

In a letter that received plenty of publicity, Patricia said she and her sister Priscilla "do not plan to discontinue our fight . . . We are very happy we are able to do this to help our city, state, and nation." Her postscript added, "My parents were here last night to get us out, but we persuaded them to let us stay."

Echoing that commitment, Barbara wrote, "We do not consider going to jail a sacrifice but a privilege. Every night we thank God we are able to help those who are denied equal rights."

Meanwhile, their lawyers appealed the convictions, claiming it was unconstitutional for any local official to impose racial discrimination against a private citizen. The lower courts denied the appeal, but the determined defendants pressed the issue until the case reached the United States Supreme Court.

The "jail-in," as it was called, brought nationwide attention to the imprisoned students. They received letters from all over, including some from other countries, expressing condemnation over the convictions. Henry hoped the jailings would force Americans to see that segregation was a moral issue that affected everyone; that if rights were denied to some citizens because of the color of their skin, then the country was not really free at all.

One morning while Henry was getting ready for another day of drudgery on the road gang, a guard told him to collect his things. Henry was being released early. No reason was given, but he assumed it was because he was so young, he was suffering from a severe cold, and also he needed to finish the school year. As grateful as he was about gaining his freedom, he vowed that, if necessary, he would do more jail time in the cause for racial equality.

The others were released after serving 49 days. Because the college students had missed so many classes at FAMU, they had to withdraw during the second semester and re-enroll for the fall term.

In late fall, CORE organized a small group of students, including Henry and the Stephens sisters, to picket downtown department stores Woolworth's, Neisner's, McCrory's, Walgreens, and Sears for three days. Walking peacefully in single file back and forth in front of the stores, the demonstrators held up signs that read WHAT IS CHRISTIAN ABOUT RACIAL DISCRIMINATION?, IMPARTIAL SERVICE FOR ALL, and THE GOLDEN RULE DOESN'T APPLY HERE. But racist thugs crowded the sidewalks and tried to provoke fights by pushing and cursing Henry and his fellow picketers. The bullies snatched signs from the picketers' hands and ripped them up. Police were on hand, witnessing the harassment, but did nothing.

In fact, they joked and conversed with the troublemakers. Henry wished he could retaliate, but he followed CORE's philosophy of nonviolence and kept picketing with his fellow demonstrators.

In March 1961 — a year after Henry and the other sit-in protestors were arrested — the Supreme Court refused to overturn their convictions. Although angry and disappointed, the students vowed to keep on fighting for equality. "We've been going up against a stone wall," Henry said. "But one day we'll break through that wall, and then there'll be freedom for all."

Tallahassee's lunch counters were finally integrated in 1963, and within a few years, the city abolished its discriminatory laws.

After graduating high school, Henry Steele attended Morehouse College in Atlanta, where he continued his activist role in the civil rights movement, including pickets, sit-ins, marches, demonstrations, rallies, and even an arrest. Following in his father's footsteps, Henry Steele then earned his divinity degree at what is now Colgate Rochester Crozer Divinity School and served as a pastor in churches in Alabama, Florida, and Georgia before retiring. He now is a volunteer at the Tallahassee Senior Center.

In honor of his father's tireless efforts in the civil rights movement — especially the bus boycott — the city of Tallahassee erected a statue of Rev. C. K. Steele when it built its new municipal bus terminal, which is also named after him. The pastor died of cancer in 1980.

Patricia Stephens suffered permanent eye damage from

the tear gas used by police during the 1961 protest march and had to wear dark glasses for the rest of her life. After marrying John Due, who became a noted civil rights attorney, Patricia served in leadership roles for CORE and the NAACP throughout the 1960s. Because her studies were constantly interrupted by protests and arrests in her fight for racial equality, Patricia didn't earn her degree from FAMU until 1967. She continued to speak out against injustice throughout her life. The mother of three, Patricia coauthored a book with her daughter, Tananarive, called Freedom in the Family: A Mother-Daughter Memoir of the Fight for Civil Rights. Patricia died in 2012 after a long bout with cancer.

ANDY HEIDELBERG AND THE NORFOLK 17

As Andrew "Andy" Heidelberg neared Norview High School, he tensed up and found it hard to breathe. Fear will do that to a 14-year-old black kid who is about to enter a previously all-white school.

It was February 2, 1959. Andy was one of 17 black students willing to brave a gauntlet of racial hostility to desegregate six schools in Norfolk, Virginia. On this day, he and six others were heading to Norview High.

All Andy could think about was the ghastly photo of Emmett Till in *Jet* magazine. Emmett, a 14-year-old Negro from Chicago, had been visiting relatives in Money, Mississippi, in 1955 when he was kidnapped, tortured, and murdered for allegedly whistling at a white woman. After his mutilated body was retrieved and returned to Chicago, his mother insisted on having an open-casket funeral so the world could see the brutality of the killing — a killing that went unpunished. Like many black-oriented publications, *Jet* published a photo of Emmett's disfigured face as he lay in his coffin.

And now as Andy walked to Norview High on the first day of school, he couldn't get that awful image of Emmett out of his mind. *Emmett was my age*, Andy thought. *They dumped his body in the river. What's going to happen to me?*

He walked around the east corner of the building, spotted a flagpole, and suddenly faced 2,500 white students, all of them, it seemed, yelling and screaming. He had never seen so many white people in one place in his life. Their faces twisted in rage and hatred, a mob of students started running toward him.

Uh-oh, Andy. They're gonna hang your butt up on that flagpole.

Growing up in segregated Norfolk, Andy never imagined that he or any other black kid would ever attend a white school. It didn't matter that the United States Supreme Court ruled in 1954 that schools had to be integrated. In Andy's mind, the chances of that happening were about the same as eating breakfast on the moon.

So in 1956 when people from the NAACP went to his home and asked him if he would be willing to help integrate the schools in Norfolk, he told them, "Sure, I'd be glad to go to a white school." It wasn't quite the truth. He just wanted to look good in front of his parents and, besides, he knew black students and white students would never, ever attend the same schools in this town.

Andy had forgotten all about his pledge until the summer of 1958, when those same NAACP folks showed up and told him he was one of more than 150 black students who had to be tested before enrolling in the white schools. Andy felt he couldn't back out, so he agreed to take the exams. He and only 16 other black students passed, and they became known as the Norfolk 17.

Over the summer, the students attended training classes to prepare them for their historic role in the city's integration. Drummed in their heads were rules of behavior: Don't start a fight. Don't hit anyone. Don't talk back. Don't retaliate even if they spit on you. Don't do anything that will give school officials an excuse to expel you.

By the end of summer, the Norfolk 17 were ready. Andy was assigned to Norview High, as were his good friend Freddy Gonsouland, Olivia Driver, Patricia Godbolt, Delores Johnson, Johnnie Rouse, and Carol Wellington. Louis Cousins was enrolled at Maury High; Betty Jean Reed, Granby High; LaVera Forbes, Edward Jordan, James "Skip" Turner, Patricia Turner, and Claudia Wellington, Norview Junior High; Lolita Portis and Reginald Young, Blair Junior High; and Geraldine Talley, Northside Junior High.

But there was no school for anyone that fall. The whites in power fought integration by launching a movement known as massive resistance. To prevent the Norfolk 17 from going to white schools in Norfolk, Virginia, Governor J. Lindsay Almond closed the six public schools they were supposed to attend as well as three schools in Arlington where four black students had planned to go. It was the only way the segregationists could keep African Americans out of the white schools — even if it meant that 13,000 white students couldn't get a public education, either.

The black schools were still open, but if the Norfolk 17 students chose to attend them, they wouldn't be able to transfer back once the white schools reopened. So the Norfolk 17 kids were in limbo, but not for long.

The NAACP started up a special school just for them in the basement of the First Baptist Church on Bute Street. Volunteer teachers taught Spanish, math, English, science, and history, and worked the students hard. Meanwhile, Andy and his pal Freddy played on an all-black community football team called the Crusaders, and led them to an undefeated season.

The Norfolk 17 attended the little school for four months before the Supreme Court ordered the state of Virginia to reopen the public schools in Norfolk and Arlington by February 2, 1959.

The night before the first day of school, Andy was worried there could be a lynching at Norview High, because there had been so many in the Deep South over the years. And then there was Emmett Till's brutal murder. No other white-on-black violence had affected him as much as Emmett's death.

The next morning, Andy's mother, Lena, came into his room and cheerily announced, "Time for you to get up, son. You've got a big day ahead of you. You have to go out there and be a pioneer for all the other kids."

She's treating this as if it's such an easy thing for me to do, he thought. *I'm scared.*

After Andy got dressed, his father, Ken, advised, "Don't worry about anything. Ignore the heckling and just smile. You'll be all right. The Lord will be with you."

As Andy walked out the door, his older brother, Kenny, Jr., said, "If anybody bothers you, I'll take care of him."

"Yeah," Andy replied, "but I'll be dead."

The day was brisk and sunny with the temperature in the low 40s when Andy and Freddy headed to school together. About a quarter of the way there, Freddy, who was a year older than Andy, asked, "Heidelberg, are you scared?" (Freddy always called Andy by his last name.)

"Scared? Nah, I ain't scared," Andy lied.

"Are you sure? Because that sure looks like sweat on your nose, and this ain't sweatin' weather."

Andy rubbed his nose. *Yeah, that's sweat all right.*

Freddy started laughing and then said, "Heidelberg, we gotta do what we gotta do."

As soon as they turned the corner, Andy gasped. In front of the school swarmed a mob of white students, yelling angrily at the first black students who already had shown up. He glanced at the flagpole and shuddered when he briefly imagined being strung up.

About 20 white students stood on the steps of the closest entrance to Andy and Freddy. One of the whites shouted, "Here come two more niggers!"

A jeering group of students broke away from the large mob and rushed toward the two African Americans. *They're gonna kill me right now,* Andy thought. *They're gonna take me to that pole, and they're gonna string me up.*

They quickly surrounded Andy and Freddy, bombarding them with vicious slurs and hateful language. Because the white kids were shouting over themselves, Andy couldn't understand much of what they were shrieking except for one word: "Nigger!" They uttered ugly chants: "Niggers over here. Niggers over there. We have niggers everywhere!" "Two, four, six, eight, we don't want to integrate!"

Newspapermen, photographers, cameramen, and TV reporters flocked around Andy and Freddy, firing one question after another: Are you frightened? How do you feel about the reception so far? Are you expecting more trouble inside? Have you been physically attacked?

The boys had been instructed not to answer questions from the news media and tried to keep walking. People were packed so tightly that Andy could feel their hot breath on his neck. He kept expecting that at any moment someone would hit him or stab him or throw a rock at him.

"Go back to Africa! Don't you understand we don't want you here! Go back to your own school, you monkey!"

No one assaulted Andy, but even if they had, it couldn't have hurt worse than the savage words aimed at him. He felt their hatred and knew that they meant every single awful thing they yelled. *How can so many people hate us when there isn't one white person here who even knows one of us?*

Finally the bell rang, and everyone headed into the school. Freddy went one way for sophomores and Andy followed the freshmen toward the auditorium. Olivia was the only other black freshman, but he couldn't find her in the throng. All he saw in the crammed hallways were white kids taunting him. Boys in front of him walked backward, facing him and shouting, "Watch out! Here comes a nigger! Don't touch him! Don't touch him!"

When Andy entered the auditorium, he was so awestruck that he momentarily shut out all the anger whirling around him. The stage was graced with full-length blue velvet drapes and the seats were soft and upholstered. He had never seen any place quite so beautiful — certainly nothing even remotely comparable to anything in the black schools. *This is magnificent,* he thought. *And it's in my new school.*

But then his ears began to burn when students in the balcony chanted, "Fe, fe, fi, fi, fo, fo, fum . . . We smell a nigger in the auditorium . . ."

As Andy walked down the aisle, he felt the angry stares of hundreds of students. *I better sit near the front, where the teachers are. Maybe they'll protect me if I get attacked, or at least prevent me from being killed.*

Seeing an empty seat in the seventh row, he eased past five students and sat down. As if on cue, everyone else in the row got up and moved. So did students in front and behind him. *Oh man, it looks like I have the plague. I don't belong here, and they sure don't want me here.* He had never felt so alone.

It was pretty much the same scene at all his classes: After Andy would find a desk, the students in front, back, and on either side of him would move away. They would continue to heckle him without any interference from the teachers.

Lunch in the cafeteria was even worse. When he entered the food line, reporters surrounded him, badgering him with questions and flashing their cameras. The attention on Andy aggravated the white students, causing them to boo and hiss.

Even though he had done nothing wrong, he was ashamed. He stared at his black hands and thought, *I wish I could be white like everyone else in here.*

His mood lightened considerably when he noticed that the women serving the food on the lunch lines were black. They were beaming with pride at his presence. Andy spoke to every one of the lunch ladies and wished he could hug and kiss them all.

After getting his tray of food, he waited for a seat to open up at a table next to the teachers. He felt safer staying as close as possible to them. At the nearest table, all the white students stared at him and then began complaining that the food stank. They rose in unison and dumped their uneaten food in the trash can. The other students in the cafeteria saw what happened and roared their approval.

Andy sat down alone at the empty table and started to eat, knowing that all eyes were on him. He hoped someone would join him, but no one did. After taking a few bites, he lost his appetite, so he got up and threw out his food.

On his way to his next class, Andy stopped outside the gym and marveled at the wall of photos of the school's past championship football teams — and there were many because the Norview Pilots were known as a perennial grid-iron powerhouse. Andy had always imagined being a high school football star. *Oh, to put on that blue-and-white uniform. How sweet would that be?*

As he dared to dream, two white students walked by. One of them snarled at him, "You can look all you want, black boy, but you ain't never gonna see a nigger on any picture on these walls."

The rest of the day was more of the same for Andy — constant harassment. When school ended, he stepped out into the sunshine and was met with a vile chant: "Hang the nigger on the flagpole! Hang the nigger on the flagpole!"

Police were there to keep the crowd under control. Andy then spotted members of the NAACP motioning him over to their car. He, Freddy, and two black girls got in. With a police escort, the car drove off past spitting students and adults.

That night, as he lay in bed, Andy told himself, *One day I'll get my picture on that wall.*

Andy assumed that after a few weeks, the racist remarks and verbal abuse would fade away. He was wrong. The overwhelming majority of white students kept piling it on the black kids day after day, making school a hurtful, lonely environment for the Norfolk 17. The NAACP kept encouraging them and reminding them of their role in history and how they were bettering themselves as well as future black youth. "Hang tough, baby," Andy was constantly reminded by family and friends. He also received letters of support from kids all over the world, praising him for his courage and boosting his confidence. He later learned that many letters sent in care of the school were returned to sender.

Like the other black students at school, Andy was the target of constant abuse. One day, a player on the baseball team met Andy in the hall, patted him on the head, and said, "Hey, Andy, what's up?" The guy stepped back, and he and his pals began to snicker. Suddenly, Andy felt a liquid trickling down his neck and then smelled an overpowering foul odor. *He got me with a liquid stink bomb! Well, I'm not taking any more junk from whitey. It's time to fight, and fight right now.*

"You know, fella, I'm gonna break your damn jaw!" Andy snapped. Just as he reached back to throw a punch, the principal blocked Andy's arm and stopped him. The principal then ordered both boys to his office.

Andy stunk so badly that the people in the office were gagging. He could barely stand it himself. The principal suspended the other boy for a week for his cruel prank, but also suspended Andy for two days for threatening the perpetrator. Because the liquid stench had seeped into his clothes, his mother had to burn them.

The daily torment was wearing him down. More than once he would stare into the mirror and ask, "Why was I born black? What kind of god would allow me to go through this kind of punishment? What did I do to deserve this?"

His mother once told him, "Always remember that you're black. If you remember that you're black, you won't be surprised when someone reminds you that you're black — and you might not like it."

Any hope that his sophomore year would be better was dashed on the first day of his return for the 1959–60 school year. For Andy and the other African Americans, the harassment from the whites continued.

In some respects, the second year was tougher than the first for Andy because he had expected it to be easier, and it wasn't. But he and his fellow black students muddled through.

Andy and his pal Freddy had starred on a Norfolk Recreation League football team that won the championship. So before the start of his junior year, Andy announced he was going to try out for Norview's football team and urged Freddy to join him.

"They're not gonna let us make the team at Norview, because we're black," Freddy said.

"Sure they will," Andy said. "We're good and they want to win."

Freddy, however, chose to return to the all-black Booker T. Washington High for his senior year so he could play football there.

During tryouts at Norview, some of the players pinched, bit, and kicked Andy. They twisted his arms and legs. They stomped and spit on him. But he refused to quit. *Some don't want to be my teammates, but they all want to win,* he told himself. *If this black boy can help them win, then they'll want me.* Andy eventually impressed some of the white players during tryouts and practice, and he felt confident he would make the team.

Before the coach made the final cut, the team scrimmaged with a squad from northern Virginia. Andy played great, scoring four touchdowns. Convinced he had proven himself, Andy was pumped when he came into the locker room to see who had made the team. After the coach posted the roster on the bulletin board, Andy scanned the list for his name, but didn't see it. Then he searched it again, certain that he had missed it on the first go-around. But no matter how many times he checked, his name wasn't on the roster.

I didn't make the team! He was crushed. There was nothing he could say, even to the few players who came up to him and told him, "Sorry, Andy. We know you should be out there with us." They knew what he knew — the cut had nothing to do with football; it was all about the color of his skin. *I want to play football and go to school and be normal and have fun. But I can't because I'm black.*

He cried on the long walk home, telling himself, *White people must really hate me* — not that he needed any reminding.

After he broke the bad news to Freddy, who had already been named Washington High's starting fullback, Freddy said, "Heidelberg, get it in your head. Norview is never gonna let blacks play on that team."

Andy's mother, though, had faith that there were better days ahead for him, saying, "The sunshine always makes you forget the rain."

To compensate for being denied the opportunity to play football, Andy participated in intramural sports and won the track championship and several other titles. But he wasn't allowed to participate in the city-wide intramural high school championship games because he was black.

During his junior year, a few white students actually engaged him in friendly conversation. But in the hallways, other students continued to insult him. *You'd think that they'd be tired of calling me the same names day after day, but I guess not.* If he accidentally bumped into a white girl, she would scream and run down the hall. The reaction always hurt and embarrassed him.

Bound and determined to make his senior year a good one, Andy once again tried out for the football team in August before the start of the 1961–62 school term. "I gotta try one more time," he told his friends. In his gut, he knew he was as good, if not better, than the players on the squad. He worked hard and went all-out. Every day, he pictured himself in that coveted blue-and-white jersey with the red and blue stripes down the pant legs.

His prospects looked bright when he began practicing with the first string and noticed players were becoming friendlier and treating him with respect. Before the final cut, the team played a scrimmage with a high school from Annandale. Andy had his best game ever, scoring a whopping seven touchdowns.

Later that day, the coach posted the roster. With his stomach tied in knots, Andy walked up to the board, held his breath, and looked for his name on the list: "Running backs — Whitley, Zongolowicz, Piercy, Spruill, Reyes, Heidelberg." Andy gasped. He had to clear his teary eyes to make sure he hadn't imagined it. *Yes, there it is! Heidelberg! I made the team! I . . . made . . . the . . . team!* Never had he felt so happy, so proud, so excited. Several players slapped him on the back and congratulated him. The walk home was the most jubilant of his young life.

On his return to classes for the start of his senior year, students were smiling at him and asking how he was doing. *Is this the same school I've been going to since my freshman year?* he wondered. *Everyone is so nice now.* For the first time ever at Norview, no one called him a racial slur. He was cheered at the pep rally. Before the first game, a white cheerleader came into the classroom, kissed him on the cheek, and said, "Good luck tonight, Andy."

When he put on that new blue-and-white uniform, he thought of his mother's words, "The sunshine always makes you forget the rain." *What a great school!*

Before the team stepped onto the field, C. J. "Zongo" Zongolowicz told Andy, "Don't worry about anything or anyone 'cause ain't nobody gonna mess with you tonight as long as I'm here." Then Kenny Whitley, the team captain, came up to Andy and said, "You better run that damn ball tonight because we're all with you."

Andy was aware that he was the "great black hope" for thousands of black fans who stood in the bleachers, counting on him to do well. He was also aware that thousands of whites were wondering if he was really that good. And there were the racists who wanted him to fail big time. If there was enormous pressure on Andy to succeed, he wasn't feeling it. He was way too excited. Walking onto the field, he prayed silently, *Dear God, bless me to play to the best of my ability. Thank you.*

He lived up to his potential. Just before the half, Andy caught a 58-yard pass for a touchdown as the fans rooted him on. The cheers seemed to have washed away all the hate that he had endured during the previous years. He reveled in the love.

Then, at the start of the second half, he received the opening kickoff, dodged a few would-be tacklers, and sprinted down the sideline. As he raced toward the end zone, he heard the fans shout, "Go, Andy, go!" It was the greatest feeling in the world when he crossed the goal line for an 81-yard touchdown return.

After the game, which Norview won 34–0, Andy was

mobbed by well-wishers, both black and white, on the field. In the locker room, reporters crowded around him — and this time, he didn't mind at all. During the questioning, a reporter asked him, "Was the reason you didn't make the team last year because you weren't big enough, that you were too light?"

"No," Andy replied. "It was because I was too dark." Everyone laughed. *Oh, man, I don't want this night to end.*

After the celebrating, his proud father told him, "It was a perfect night, but I'm still upset because there was a white fan who kept yelling, 'Give the ball to that nigger!'"

"Dad, he's a fan. That's how the whites talk."

"I don't care. I don't like him talking that way."

The next week, Norview put its nearly 4-year, 37-game win streak on the line against champions E. C. Glass High in Lynchburg, Virginia, 200 miles away in what was considered an area of rabid bigotry.

On the way to the night game, the Norview team bus stopped about 60 miles from Lynchburg for a 4 P.M. dinner. Because the restaurant wasn't quite ready, the players strolled toward the center of town. They were feeling loose and joking around. As they turned the corner, Andy noticed the name above the courthouse: Prince Edward County. *I read something about this county, but I can't remember what,* he thought.

One of his teammates clutched Andy's arm and said, "Do you know where we are? We're in Farmville, the county seat of Prince Edward County."

"So?" Andy replied.

"Andy, they hate Negroes so much they closed all the public schools here a couple of years ago rather than integrate — and those schools are still closed."

"What's going to happen to Andy if people get wind he's in town?" a teammate asked.

Whitley whistled for the players to listen up. "They don't like colored people here, and they mean business," he said. "We're going to turn around and go back to the restaurant. Andy, you get in the middle and let's surround him so they can't easily spot him." Trying to stay calm, Andy kept himself in the protective shield of his 60 teammates as they walked a half mile back to the restaurant without incident.

Inside, the players relaxed and began cracking jokes again. Andy was sitting at a booth with Zongo, Kenny, and another teammate. "That was close," said Kenny. "You don't want to be a Negro in this town."

Buck Moody, the assistant coach, walked over to their table, looking grim. He said, "Andy, they aren't going to let you eat here in the dining area. In fact, they won't serve any of us if you're out here."

Some of the players in the nearby booth chortled. One of them said, "You shouldn't joke like that, Coach."

Moody shook his head. "I'm not joking. This is serious. They won't feed us with you here, Andy. They said you can eat in the kitchen."

Once again, Andy's mother's words popped into his head, only it had nothing to do with sunshine and everything to do about being reminded he was black. *I'm back to being a nigger again*. Tears welled up in Andy's eyes. "Okay, Coach, I'll go."

"I'm sorry, Andy," said Moody.

With every step toward the kitchen, Andy felt the sting of prejudice jab at his heart. He glanced at his teammates and could tell from the look in their eyes they felt badly for him.

When he walked into the kitchen, he was greeted by a black man and a black woman who had laid out a table laden with all kinds of food. They were flashing big smiles that reminded him of the lunch ladies on his first day at Norview. They were so proud of him. "Come on in here, son," said the man. "We're gonna feed you good like a king."

About a minute after Andy sat down, the kitchen door opened and in walked Zongo and Kenny. "If you're eatin' in the kitchen, then we're eatin' in the kitchen," Zongo declared. They pulled up chairs and enjoyed a feast that left them stuffed. Andy was incredibly appreciative of his two backfield teammates.

When the meal was over and everyone returned to the bus, Kenny told Andy loud enough for everyone to hear, "If any other restaurant makes Andy eat in the kitchen, I'm going with him because we ate real well." The players laughed.

Andy felt like he was a member of a real team — even more so now than after the first game. But there was no escaping the ugly specter of racism. Someone had brought on board a local newspaper that had a story about the upcoming game. Accompanying the article was a photo of an E. C. Glass player with a caption that had a message for the Norview team: "We're gonna beat you and your nigger tonight."

And they did, too, walloping Norview 21–0. In the Pilots'

first loss in four years, the E. C. Glass players beat up on Andy and cursed him on every play. But he took it in stride, figuring it was all part of the game.

With Andy as a star running back and defensive back, Norview won the rest of its games, finishing the year 9-1. In the final contest of his high school career, Andy rushed for more than 100 yards and scored on a 54-yard touchdown run to help his team win Virginia's Eastern District Championship.

Now that he was finally accepted by the student body, Andy reveled in the rest of his senior year, making many new friends. He realized that the football season had achieved something that he could never have accomplished by just attending class. He had helped bring whites and blacks together.

Although he helped narrow the racial divide in Norfolk, it was far from closed. The black students weren't allowed to attend prom and, despite his stellar record on the gridiron, Andy was passed over for any city-wide awards.

Still, there were some exceptional victories. One that he cherished came at the end of the school year when everyone was signing one another's yearbooks. A white student, Don Lane, wrote in Andy's yearbook: "Before I met you, colored people were niggers. But now I realize that they are humans. Thank you for the opportunity to see the light, for you are a swell guy and I wish you a heck of a lot of luck and happiness in the future."

There was also another personal victory that held special meaning for Andy. It was a photo of him in a football uniform on the wall at Norview High School.

*　　*　　*

Andrew "Andy" Heidelberg graduated from Norfolk State University and spent 17 years in the banking industry, where he served as vice president and corporate manager of several major banks in the United States and England. He later served as assistant treasurer and chief deputy treasurer for the city of Hampton, Virginia.

A deacon at Temple Beth El in Suffolk, Virginia, Heidelberg continues to speak at various forums and on broadcasts about the black experience and desegregation in sports. He wrote a book about his experience called The Norfolk 17: A Personal Narrative on Desegregation in Norfolk, Virginia, 1958–62.

Heidelberg, whose two daughters graduated from Norview High, lives with his wife, Luressa, in Hampton.

"All seventeen of us black kids had different stories to tell," he says. "We were ordinary black kids chosen to do an extraordinary task during an extraordinary time. I think we did a hell of a job."

JANICE WESLEY AND THE CHILDREN'S CRUSADE

Hundreds of black teenagers who had been walking peacefully in a downtown protest march suddenly found themselves blasted by powerful streams of water from high-pressure fire hoses. The drenched students locked arms with one another and tried desperately to hold their ground. But it was impossible to withstand the force of the hoses gripped by firemen who had been ordered to set the water pressure to a level that would peel the bark off a tree.

Some of the kids were ripped from one another's grasps and flattened. Others who were doubled over or cowering with their hands over their heads were helpless against the fierce torrents that rolled them down the street and side-walks like bowling balls.

Another wave of marching youths approached, and as they turned the corner, they were slammed against walls by the same fire hoses. The water barrage tore shirts off guys in the front of the group and shoved several girls over the hoods of parked cars.

Kids who were lucky enough to dodge the torrents still faced other perilous hazards. Snarling, barking police dogs chased after them, inflicting bites on legs and arms and ripping clothes off the slowest demonstrators.

This was the second day of the Children's Crusade, an extraordinary protest of thousands of high school, middle school, and grade school students. They were attempting to do what the adults had so far failed to do — force an end to segregation in Birmingham, Alabama.

On the first day, May 2, 1963, more than 700 students were arrested for marching. One of those was 16-year-old Janice Wesley.

Living in a black neighborhood and attending black schools and a black church, Janice had little contact with white people in Birmingham, which was considered one of the most segregated large cities in the South. Racial inequality wasn't a big issue for her, because she had accepted the facts of Birmingham life. She and her eight siblings understood that whites were more privileged than black people, that African Americans could spend their money in downtown stores but were not hired there or served at lunch counters, and that white police officers had the power — which they often used — to hassle the black community.

Janice's mother, Katye Ruth Wesley, was active in voter registration and street improvements in the black neighborhoods, but wasn't involved in protests. Katye worked in the cafeteria of all-white Woodlawn High School at a time when black students were attempting to enroll there. One day, white students hanged an effigy of a black student out the library window. Katye was so disgusted that she took off her apron, walked home, and refused to work there again.

As a young teenager, Janice was more interested in boys, romance novels, and rock 'n' roll than in the civil rights movement. But in March 1963, when she was 15, Janice had an awakening. She had gone with a friend to the annex of Pilgrim Baptist Church to hear James Bevel, of the SCLC, speak about racial injustice.

During Bevel's talk to the teenagers, she learned that while her all-black school, Ullman High, had just one electric typewriter for students, the whites-only Phillips High had three *rooms* of electric typewriters. And she learned her school received the discarded books and equipment from all-white Ramsay High.

"Ever wonder how much white folks pay for a hot dog and Coke when they sit down at the nice lunch counter at J. J. Newberry's department store?" Bevel continued. "Twenty-seven cents. And how much do you pay for a hot dog and Coke — which you can only get after passing the lunch counter and going up to the fourth floor and then eating while standing up? Twenty-seven cents."

I pay the same as whites, but they get to sit in comfy seats on the first floor and I can't? Janice thought, her resentment building. *They're treating me wrong!*

"If you want to do something about this inequality, you can," Bevel told the students. "Your parents can't get too involved because if they try, they will get arrested or they will lose their jobs or get hurt. If you get arrested, it'll cost you a few days away from school. But what does that matter? You're getting a second-class education, anyway."

From then on, Janice was committed to the cause. She didn't tell her parents what she was doing, because she thought they would try to discourage her. Her father worked in a steel mill and her mother was an insurance agent for a black-owned company. At the time, many African Americans who held jobs in Birmingham were afraid that the civil rights movement would hurt them because of white backlash. The black community tended to remain apathetic to the SCLC's lunch counter sit-ins, pickets, and marches that protested the city's white supremacy and segregation laws. Even Dr. Martin Luther King, Jr.'s, arrest in April during a peaceful demonstration didn't generate enough indignation to jumpstart the stagnating movement in Birmingham.

But then Bevel came up with the idea of the Children's Crusade. So the SCLC and Rev. Fred Shuttlesworth's Alabama Christian Movement for Human Rights recruited young people from ages 6 to 18. Janice volunteered. She attended youth workshops where she and other students met with leaders of the SCLC, often in the basement of the Sixteenth Street Baptist Church or on the lawn of the A. G. Gaston Motel. They were given lessons on nonviolent direct action by Bevel, Shuttlesworth, Dr. King, Andrew Young, and other civil rights activists.

The students learned about successes and failures of sit-ins and protest marches in other Southern cities. They were taught freedom songs and how to respond nonviolently to racist hostility during demonstrations. After weeks of training, the young people were ready to take the lead — and face jail time — in the struggle for racial equality.

On Thursday morning, May 2, 1963, Janice woke up with freedom on her mind and excitement in her soul. This was the day when students would walk out of school, gather at the Sixteenth Street Baptist Church, and march downtown. Organizers called it C-Day for Confrontation Day, but the students referred to it as D-Day, named after the WWII invasion.

As she got dressed that morning, Janice thought, *We will get our freedom*. Humming the freedom songs she had learned over the past few weeks, she packed her purse with everything she thought she'd need for an overnight stay in jail — toothbrush, toothpaste, soap, underwear. She also borrowed her sister's jacket because she had been told it would be cold behind bars.

At school, Janice, who had a good GPA, had concerns about how her teachers would react to the students skipping classes. To her first-period teacher, she asked, "If the kids walk out, will you fail us?"

"Well, if everybody walks, then there's nobody to fail," the teacher replied.

I take that to mean the teachers won't punish us, Janice thought.

The vast majority of students had agreed to leave. Those who chose to remain behind did so because they were afraid their parents would lose their jobs. As one classmate told Janice, "I wish I could join you, but I can't. My dad is a chauffeur for a white man who told him, 'I better not see your kids' names in the paper, or you won't work for me anymore.' "

After first period, students poured out of school. Janice spotted the principal standing by the door, observing but doing nothing to stop the flood of kids exiting the building. They walked two miles to the Sixteenth Street Baptist Church, which was the staging area for black students from other schools to gather before marching downtown.

On the way to the church, some students had transistor radios and were listening to the black disc jockeys talking in code like, "We're gonna jump and shout; gonna turn it out! We're gonna have a party in the park." They were referring to Kelly Ingram Park next to the church. The DJs reported on the number of students leaving the various schools, which totaled close to 1,000.

Inside the church, the students were given last-minute reminders what to do if they were harassed by the police or racists: kneel, pray, sing freedom songs. Students were to march in groups of 50 to City Hall. Janice was in the first group, which left the church walking in pairs and singing "We Shall Overcome." Their young voices were strong, sending tingles of exhilaration down Janice's spine. To her, it sounded as if the whole world was singing. *God is on our side*, she thought.

Before reaching their destination, however, they were blocked by a menacing line of police officers. Speaking through a megaphone, an officer told the students, "You are in violation of a city ordinance. You cannot parade without a permit. If you disperse immediately, nothing will happen to you. If you don't, you are going to jail."

Janice felt what most of the kids felt — intimidated. She wasn't accustomed to disobeying an adult, especially a white cop with a pistol on his hip and a billy club in his hand. *Should I go or stay?* she wondered. Then she heard a student behind her begin singing, *"We are not afraid. We are not afraid. We are not afraid today . . ."* Everyone in the group joined in, which gave Janice and the others the courage to remain rooted and ignore the cop's warning.

The police then made good on their threat. They herded the students — who submitted to arrest without resistance — into paddy wagons. Janice and her friends were not scared. Quite the opposite. They were stomping their feet, clapping their hands, and singing loudly. While her paddy wagon was getting filled up with more protestors, she and the others began swaying back and forth, trying to rock the vehicle so hard it would tip over. They didn't succeed.

When Janice was asked by an officer why the kids hated whites, she replied, "We don't hate white people. We don't even know any. We hate the system they created. That's what we're protesting about."

The demonstrators were taken to the family court building, where they were charged with marching without a permit. Then they were put on buses — which were usually used to transport white students to school — and taken to the county jail. It was a thrill for Janice because it was the first time that she had ridden in a yellow school bus and the first time that she had sat in the front. The irony wasn't lost on her that these milestones occurred only because she was on her way to jail.

When the first 50 students were hauled away, a second group of 50 left the church and headed toward City Hall, but they were arrested, too. The pattern was repeated over and over until more than 700 students were put behind bars. Some, including Janice, were put in a dormitory at a nearby arena.

On the second day, about a thousand more students continued the protest. The young marchers left the church and walked across Kelly Ingram Park, chanting "Freedom! Freedom! Freedom!" Determined to prevent them from reaching downtown, Public Safety Commissioner Eugene "Bull" Connor impeded their way with an army of firemen, who were holding high-pressure hoses, and law enforcement officers, some with police dogs.

Through a portable loudspeaker, Police Captain G. V. Evans told the students, "Disperse, or you'll get wet." When they bravely kept marching, Connor ordered the firemen to blast them. Black spectators, who minutes earlier had been cheering on the youths, were furious over the cruel water assault and began yelling. So, on Connor's command, the firemen turned the hoses on the adults. In retaliation, the bystanders began throwing rocks and bottles at the police. Connor then called for the German shepherd police dogs to chase them.

Although the students remained nonviolent, James Bevel frantically tried to curb the angry adults from injuring anyone. He kept shouting, "If any cops get hurt, we're going to lose this fight!"

Kids who had been arrested in the second day of

demonstrations and hauled to the arena gave Janice and the other prisoners shocking accounts of the brutality they endured. Some of the new arrivals were still soaked from being hosed by firefighters; some were sporting bruises, cuts, and scratches; and others showed where they had been bitten or had clothing torn by the police dogs. Reports filtered in that several children had been taken to the hospital for treatment of injuries they received from the police and firefighters.

That evening at a mass meeting at the Sixteenth Street Baptist Church, Dr. King gave a speech explaining why the Children's Crusade must continue. He told parents of the young protestors, "Don't worry about your children. They are going to be all right. Don't hold them back if they want to go to jail, for they are not only doing a job for themselves, but for all of America and for all of mankind."

On Sunday, three days after her arrest, Janice and some of her fellow students were released from police custody. When her parents picked her up at the arena, they weren't happy. Her mother scolded her for participating in the Children's Crusade, but made it clear she was upset because of the danger the kids had faced. "I had no idea of how bad it would get," Janice responded. "I didn't have any reason to believe anyone would hurt me."

Despite the arrests on Thursday and the mayhem dealt to students on Friday, the Children's Crusade continued into the next week with even more arrests, including that of Janice's 17-year-old brother, Alvin. He spent a week in jail before he was released.

When he returned home, he told Janice, "I was concerned about how worried Mom was when you were in jail, so I thought I better go down and see what was going on. I would have been protesting with you on Thursday, but I couldn't miss spring football practice. You know how important football is to me. But after you got arrested, football wasn't as important to me, not with knowing my sister was in jail. I didn't want to do less than what you had done. So I was part of Monday's demonstration and got arrested."

By now, photos and footage of children being knocked down by high-pressure fire hoses, attacked by police dogs, and clubbed by law enforcement officers had appeared in newspapers and on television throughout the world. The disturbing images ignited a firestorm of condemnation against Birmingham officials and generated demands that the federal government get involved. It had been federal policy to let local law enforcement handle civil rights protests. Unable to turn a blind eye any longer, President John F. Kennedy sent Burke Marshall, assistant attorney general for civil rights, to Birmingham to broker a deal between the SCLC and local officials.

Meanwhile, against a backdrop of sporadic rioting by adults, wave after wave of new students peacefully marched in protest, courageously facing water hoses and police dogs before ending up in jail. More than 2,500 youths were arrested. The *New York Times* slammed Birmingham's callous mistreatment of the students as "a national disgrace." President Kennedy called the photos of the brutality "shameful," adding that they made him "sick."

A week after the Children's Crusade started, the SCLC ended the daily demonstrations in exchange for the city's promise to desegregate downtown stores, hire black clerks, release all protestors from jail, and remove Connor — who became an instant nationwide symbol of Southern racial bigotry — from his position.

Janice and her fellow students were proud that the Children's Crusade forced the city fathers to begin the integration process. But out of spite, the Birmingham Board of Education announced that all students who participated in the demonstrations would be either suspended or expelled from school. The SCLC and the NAACP then went to the local federal district court, asking the judge to overrule the board's decision. But he sided with the board. So the SCLC and the NAACP took the issue to the Fifth Circuit Court of Appeals, which not only reversed the decision but criticized the board of education for its vindictive actions.

Over the next several months, segregation in Birmingham slowly began to crumble. But with progress came more violence. Ku Klux Klansmen blew up a black-owned hotel, lobbed tear gas canisters into several stores that integrated, and tossed dynamite at the houses of local black leaders. This pattern of racist-inspired explosions gave the city an ugly reputation . . . and an even uglier nickname: Bombingham.

And then it got worse.

Sunday, September 15, started out as a picture-perfect bright morning. Janice woke up to the aroma of bacon frying and biscuits baking. At the breakfast table, her father offered a blessing, and each child, as was the Wesley household custom, quoted a Bible verse before eating. Once the table was cleared, Janice and her siblings got dressed for Sunday school and strolled three blocks to their church, South Elyton Baptist Church.

Unexpectedly, during the middle of the service, their pastor, Rev. Moreland Lanier, strode to the pulpit and told the congregation, "I have some terrible news. The Sixteenth Street Baptist Church has been bombed." Worshippers gasped and screamed. "There are casualties." The church echoed with more anguished shouts. "We don't know if our church is next, so I advise everyone to leave quickly but orderly and go home — and pray."

The announcement stunned Janice and left her in a bewildering state of disbelief. Her body began to shake, first from fear and then anger and finally flat-out grief. *They bombed a church on a Sunday morning? They would only do that if they were trying to hurt somebody. This is crazy. This is horrible.*

The grim facts began to filter throughout the black community. A box of dynamite that had been planted near the church's front steps exploded just as 26 children were walking into the basement assembly room to hear a sermon called "The Love That Forgives." Killed were four young girls — Denise McNair, 11; Addie Mae Collins, 14; Carole Robertson, 14; and Cynthia Wesley, 14. The other children were injured, many seriously. The blast blew a hole in the church's rear wall and shattered all the stained glass windows except for one that was damaged but still in place — the one showing Christ leading a group of little children.

After Janice and her family returned home, the phone kept ringing constantly from friends and relatives who were crying and upset because they thought that the Wesley girl who was killed was Janice. Throughout the rest of that terrible day, Janice heard her parents say repeatedly on the phone, "It's not our child."

But it was somebody's child — someone whom Janice knew well. Cynthia Wesley and Janice shared the same last name but were not related. However, they were friends who enjoyed orchestra together and went to Ullman High. Janice had gone to lawn parties thrown in Cynthia's honor by her adoptive parents. All Janice could picture in her mind was a smart, pretty girl who smiled a lot — a friend she would never see again. Janice was devastated because she had never known anybody close to her age who had died, let alone been murdered.

The tragic news was hard for Janice to process, especially when she learned the identities of the other fatalities. She knew the families of two of the other three girls. Carole's father had been Janice's band teacher and Denise's dad was the family's milkman.

They didn't deserve to die, Janice told herself. *They didn't do anything to make someone hate them. All they did was go to Sunday school. And now they're dead. How could somebody do this? How could someone kill innocent children?* She felt overwhelmed, sad, and sickened by the murders. But then another feeling crowded into her troubled psyche. She felt guilty. She kept thinking of all the times she and other students attended protest training sessions in the basement of the Sixteenth Street Baptist Church. *Am I partly responsible for their deaths? Maybe if we hadn't used the church for training or as a staging area for our demonstrations, maybe Cynthia and the other girls would still be alive.*

Janice didn't talk to her friends or family about her feelings. Nobody really discussed such personal matters back then. They conversed about the senseless crime and equal rights, but not about the hurt they all felt. So Janice kept her thoughts and feelings bottled up inside. She had done such a good job of blocking them that she couldn't bring herself to cry, not even at the funeral for three of the girls, which was attended by 8,000 mourners. (The family of the fourth girl held a private service.) There were so many people at the funeral and so many dignitaries who spoke, including Dr. King, that Janice didn't have a chance to grieve.

Eventually, when the heartache began to diminish, Janice made a pledge to herself to continue the fight for racial justice. *Those girls are not going to die in vain,* she vowed. *I'm going to do what I can to ensure that our rights aren't trampled on. I owe it to those who made the ultimate sacrifice to get those rights won.*

The Children's Crusade — and the nationwide outrage over the violence aimed at the young people of Birmingham — energized the civil rights movement and awakened Americans to press legislators for passage of laws assuring equality for every citizen, regardless of race. The young protestors' courage helped lead to the Civil Rights Act of 1964 and the Voting Rights Act of 1965.

Although Dr. Martin Luther King, Jr., faced criticism for exposing young people to danger during the Children's Crusade, he maintained that their involvement helped them develop a "sense of their own stake in freedom." He later wrote, "Looking back, it is clear that the introduction of

Birmingham's children into the campaign was one of the wisest moves we made. It brought a new impact to the crusade, and the impetus that we needed to win the struggle."

The bombing of the Sixteenth Street Baptist Church remained unsolved for years. The FBI suspected four Ku Klux Klansmen: Robert "Dynamite Bob" Chambliss, Thomas E. Blanton, Jr., Herman Cash, and Bobby Frank Cherry. But federal charges were not filed because of a lack of witness cooperation and physical evidence.

However, Alabama Attorney General Bill Baxley reopened the case and brought Chambliss to trial in 1977. Chambliss was convicted of the murder of Denise McNair and sentenced to life in prison. He died eight years later. In 2001, Blanton was tried and convicted of four counts of murder and sentenced to life in prison. The following year, Cherry was found guilty of the murders and received a life sentence. Cash died in 1994 without having been charged.

Throughout school, Janice Wesley continued her involvement in the civil rights movement. She attended Miles College, where she earned a bachelor's degree in biology and later earned a master's and educational specialist degrees in counseling from the University of Alabama at Birmingham. She and her husband, Rufus D. Kelsey, have two children and five grandchildren.

Janice Wesley Kelsey enjoyed a 33-year career in education as a teacher, counselor, and an elementary school principal. Since retiring, Mrs. Kelsey has become an independent educational consultant, working with agencies such as the African American Studies Program at UAB, the Birmingham Civil

Rights Institute, and United Way of Central Alabama. She also manages her church's after-school and summer programs.

"For years following the bombing of the Sixteenth Street Baptist Church, I did not talk to anyone about what I felt," she says. "In fact thirty years passed before anyone asked me to share what I remembered about 1963. After thinking about it, I cried. Now, more than fifty years after the fact, I still cry sometimes because it still hurts."

But much has changed in Birmingham. The residents elected an African American mayor and a city council with a black majority, and the school system hired a black superintendent. Janice Wesley Kelsey's brother, Dr. Michael W. Wesley, Jr., became a principal at Woodlawn High — the same school where their mother had once worked before quitting over a malicious racial prank. Kelly Ingram Park, which often served as a staging area for protests, features several sculptures commemorating the civil rights movement. Nearby is the Birmingham Civil Rights Institute, a large interpretive museum and research center that depicts the struggles of the movement in the 1950s and 1960s.

"We took a stand in 1963," says Janice. "I hope that our efforts will remind today's young people that, no matter your age, you can find the courage to stand up for what you believe in and win wars through nonviolence. You don't need to be a leader to make a difference. You need to be an activist who understands that it's your responsibility to make life better for your community and your country. And it's your responsibility to know history so we don't repeat the mistakes of the past."

LUVAGHN BROWN AND THE GREENWOOD STRUGGLE

It was just his second night in Greenwood, Mississippi — one of the most brutal, violent towns in the state — and already 17-year-old Luvaghn Brown was running for his life.

As a gang of armed racists seeking to bash heads was stomping up the stairway toward the second-floor office of the local civil rights field office, Luvaghn and two fellow activists were inside making their escape. Rushing to the back room, they leaped out a window and onto a roof. With the hatemongers only seconds behind them, the three young men knew there was only one way out of this dilemma. They would have to slide down the pole of a TV antenna and hope there weren't any waiting thugs lurking in the dark to assault them.

This wasn't the kind of welcome that Luvaghn was picturing when he arrived in town the day before, on August 16, 1962, with Tougaloo College student Lawrence Guyot, 22 (who was called by just his last name). They had come to Greenwood to help Sam Block, 23, a SNCC field secretary, spearhead a voter registration drive. Sam was still sporting bruises from an attack three days earlier by three white men who demanded he get out of town.

During Luvaghn's first night in Greenwood, he attended a meeting with Sam, Guyot, and several local volunteers at the office located above a café. Because a wave of terror perpetrated by white extremists had frightened the black community, the young activists were aware that their own lives were in danger. Even though they knew that a drive-by shooting could happen at any moment, they carried on. With the shades pulled down, they made plans to canvass neighborhoods and look for black adults willing to attempt to register to vote.

Trying to give Luvaghn and Guyot a sense of the difficulty they faced, Sam explained that he had been knocking on doors alone since June. "I canvassed every day and every night until I found about seven or eight people who were brave enough to try to register," Sam said. "I escorted them to the courthouse. It was my first time there, and the sheriff asked me, 'Where you from?' I told him, 'Well, I'm a native Mississippian.' He said, 'I know you ain't from 'round here, 'cause I know every nigger and his mammy.' I said, 'Well, you might know all the niggers, but do you know any colored people?' He got angry, spat in my face, and told me, 'I don't want to see you in town anymore. The best thing for you is to pack your clothes and get out and don't never come back.' I said, 'Well, Sheriff, if you don't want to see me here, I think the best thing for you to do is pack your clothes and get out of town, because I'm here to stay. I came here to do a job, and I'm going to do it.'"

The next day Luvaghn, Guyot, Sam, and several volunteers spread out and talked to about 100 black residents. Only ten said they would go to the SNCC office later to be escorted to the courthouse. But just three ever showed up.

Luvaghn and Guyot went back to talk to the other seven. The residents confessed that they had changed their minds because they were too scared.

After Guyot escorted three black women to the courthouse, he returned to the office disappointed. "The chief of police stopped us and cursed and threatened the ladies," Guyot told Luvaghn. "They were too frightened to go inside. The intimidation was too great."

Later that night, Luvaghn, Guyot, and Sam looked out their office window and noticed a police cruiser motoring slowly past the building. Following behind was a car loaded with white men, staring up at them.

Sam turned off the lights. Moments later, the trio saw the squad car drive by again, but this time the tailing vehicle stopped in front of the building and out stepped six men carrying chains, bats, and guns.

Turning away from the window, Sam said, "We need to leave right now!"

Knowing that their main exit was down the stairs and out the front door, Luvaghn said, "If we go out through the front, we'll likely get beaten to death. How will we get out of here?"

"Follow me," Sam whispered. They went to the back room and opened a window that looked out onto the roof of an adjoining building in the back. Hearing men's footsteps thundering up the stairway, the three activists climbed out the window and onto the roof. In desperation, they slid down the pole of a television antenna, skinning up their hands, before leaping to the ground. On the final jump, Sam twisted his ankle badly, so Luvaghn and Guyot assisted him as they escaped through the alleys to the home of a supporter who gave them refuge.

When the trio returned the next day, they found the office door had been bashed in. The room was trashed and certain files — some with names of black residents who were willing to register — were missing. The black landlord showed up and said that he was facing an arrest on bogus charges if he didn't evict SNCC. "I'm sorry," he said, "but you'll have to find another place for your office. The whites here are just too powerful."

Luvaghn was no stranger to racial violence and no fan of whites in general.

Growing up in a poverty-stricken neighborhood in segregated Jackson, Mississippi, Luvaghn left an abusive family life when he was a high school senior. He survived on the streets by relying on his smarts and a strong work ethic. So bright that he skipped a grade, Luvaghn graduated at age 16 in 1961. The homeless teen slept wherever he could, usually at a friend's house. Some of his siblings — he had eight — would bring him clothes or he would sneak back home to eat and see his mother while his stepfather was at work. Luvaghn always had a few dollars in his pocket by doing day jobs such as delivering groceries or unloading trucks in downtown Jackson.

He sometimes worked at a white-owned business that sold food, beer, and blocks of ice. He was a good employee, but he was also black, which meant he couldn't use the only bathroom in the store. For his bathroom break, he had to walk to the gas station up the street. The same was true if he wanted to quench his thirst, because he wasn't allowed to drink from the store's water fountain.

Luvaghn knew that if he dared object to these unfair racial customs, bad things could happen to him — getting beat up, thrown in jail, or even killed. The vicious 1955 murder of 14-year-old Emmett Till was still fresh in his mind. So he remained careful when dealing with white people.

Even though he felt that African Americans were treated like second-class citizens in the Jim Crow South, Luvaghn never felt inferior to whites. But festering inside him was a growing hatred of them because they held all the power. Heightening that hostility was his own rage stemming from years of mental and physical abuse at the hands of his stepfather. Because the two most dominant emotions that he felt were fear and anger, he was prone to getting into fistfights.

He wondered if life for him and other black youths would ever change. Then he met SNCC members James Bevel and Bernard Lafayette, Jr., who were recruiting young people for the civil rights movement in Mississippi.

Although Luvaghn was encouraged to see some black people challenge discrimination in the state, SNCC's philosophy of nonviolence was a foreign concept to him. "I don't see the point of doing something for the cause that would allow white people to beat on me without me fighting back," he told his leaders. But he kept listening to them and over time he began to buy into much of what they believed. *Maybe their ideas will work,* he thought. *Maybe I really can help bring some changes around here.*

One day he was walking downtown with his friend Jimmy Travis, who had attended SNCC meetings with him, when they passed Woolworth's, which barred black people from eating at its lunch counter. On the spur of the moment, Luvaghn said, "Let's go in and order a sandwich."

That sounded fine with Jimmy, so the two entered the store and sat down at the lunch counter. "We'd like something to eat, please," Luvaghn told the startled waitress.

"This is for whites only, so you have to leave right now," she snapped.

When the boys didn't move, the manager called the police. The officers arrived and ordered the two to get out. They refused, so they were arrested and tossed in jail. As he stewed behind bars, Luvaghn realized that he had broken three rules he had been taught growing up: Don't challenge whites, don't anger whites, don't mess with the police. Fear kicked into overdrive for him because none of their friends or SNCC people knew what had happened to the boys. *Bad things could happen to me,* he thought. Luckily, they didn't, and the two were eventually bailed out.

From then on, Luvaghn was dedicated to the movement, believing it was his best chance to strike back at white supremacy. But just as important, he had found a home among the devoted, confident activists — including several white people from Northern states — and had bonded with them. For the first time in his life, he felt he was part of something big and influential and worthwhile.

But he faced constant reminders that the whites in power in Jackson were not willing to give up their bigoted ways.

One day, Luvaghn was walking down the street with Joan Trumpauer, a 19-year-old white Freedom Rider and SNCC worker, when the cops ordered them in a squad car and took them to the police station. There, Captain J. L. Ray, who knew Luvaghn, scolded him for being seen in public with Joan. "You shouldn't be walking down the street with a white woman," Ray told him. "There are people in this jail, black and white, who would kill you for that." Fortunately, the two weren't charged. Ray sent Joan on her way through the front door and Luvaghn out the back door with the warning, "Make sure you aren't seen together in public."

In the spring of 1962, James Bevel's wife, Diane Nash, a member of SNCC, was arrested in Jackson for "contributing to the delinquency of minors." Her crime: teaching the techniques of nonviolence to black teenagers. She was found guilty and sentenced to two years in prison. Even though she was four months pregnant and could have posted bond and been free pending an appeal, Diane insisted on serving her time. She told Judge Russell Moore, "I no longer can cooperate with the evil and corrupt court system in this state. Since my child will be a black child born in Mississippi, he will be born in prison whether I am in jail or not." (Diane was released after a few weeks behind bars.)

At her trial, Luvaghn and fellow student activist Jesse Harris decided to challenge the courtroom's segregated seating policy by sitting in the white section. Moore ordered them to move to the "colored side," but they refused. Naturally, they were arrested.

On the day of their trial, Luvaghn asked Moore to recuse (disqualify) himself because he was the one who had them arrested. The judge replied, "I will do no such thing." When Luvaghn demanded to know why, the irritated judge barked, "I don't have to explain anything to you." Moments later, Luvaghn and Jesse were each fined $100 and sentenced to 30 days hard labor at the Hinds County Penal Farm. Because neither defendant had enough money for the fine, they were told they would have to work it off by staying longer in prison.

The two were soon put on separate road gangs lorded over by sadistic guards who took special pleasure in torturing civil rights activists.

One day, Luvaghn was cutting brush in the hot Mississippi sun when his hands cramped up so badly that he was forced to stop.

His shotgun-toting guard, Captain Wright, bellowed, "Nigger, get back to work!"

"I can't, Cap'n," Luvaghn said. "My hands have frozen up on me and they hurt real bad."

"I'll show you hurt," Wright growled. He snapped off a fat stick from a tree, ordered several prisoners to hold Luvaghn down on the ground and then beat him. After Wright was through, he shouted, "Now get back to work!"

Reeling from the thrashing and still suffering from painful hand cramps, Luvaghn muttered that he was in no shape to continue. Wright exploded and gave him another licking with the stick.

Nursing his cuts and bruises from the double thrashing, Luvaghn was back on the road gang the next day. He was clearing more brush when he heard Wright yell, "Brown!" Rather than answer "Yes, sir, Cap'n" as prisoners were supposed to do when being addressed, Luvaghn replied in a snappy tone, "What?"

His disrespectful response infuriated Wright, so when Luvaghn turned around, he found himself staring down the barrel of a loaded revolver. Wright aimed his gun directly between Luvaghn's eyes and snarled, "I could kill you out here right now, and nobody would give a damn."

"Yes, sir, Cap'n," replied Luvaghn, who was terrified because Wright's threat rang true.

After several tense seconds, Wright holstered his weapon and Luvaghn went back to work. Eventually, the guard became less belligerent and one day told him, "Listen, kid, you're messin' up your life hangin' 'round them outside agitators. They're gonna get you killed. They don't care about you. Why don't you do somethin' meanin'ful instead of causin' trouble with all this civil rights stuff. You ain't gonna change things 'round here nohow."

"Yes, sir, Cap'n," Luvaghn said, but all the time thinking, *When I get out of here, I'm going right back to doing what I've been doing for the cause.*

Jesse fared worse than Luvaghn did in prison. A guard whipped him with a piece of hose. Another time, Jesse was beaten with a stick, handcuffed, and taken to the county jail where he was kept in a sweat box — a tiny, windowless cell — for days and given a measly diet of bread and water.

After 42 grueling days in prison, the boys were released. Despite his fear of bodily harm, Luvaghn volunteered for SNCC to work in dangerous Greenwood, Mississippi, on a new voters' rights project. It didn't escape him that the town was only a 25-minute ride to where Emmett Till had been killed.

As the unofficial capital of the cotton-rich Mississippi Delta, Greenwood was the seat of Leflore County. It was run by an iron-fisted white citizens' council, which, along with the Ku Klux Klan, had thwarted black people from registering to vote through raw violence, threatening intimidation, and heartless firings and evictions. The white power structure's brazen tactics had kept most African Americans uneducated, impoverished, and politically helpless.

In the early 1960s, black families in the Delta earned an average of only $27 a week or $1,400 a year (the equivalent of about $11,000 in 2014). On average, they received about five years of public education compared to eleven years for whites. More than 80 percent of black people lived in substandard houses — typically tar-paper shacks lit by a single lightbulb — and often were charged more for electricity than the whites who lived in much bigger, nicer homes.

Even though nearly two-thirds of the county's adults were black, only 2 percent were registered to vote, compared to almost 100 percent of eligible whites. During the 7 years before Luvaghn arrived there, only 40 black people had been allowed to register to vote, compared to 1,664 whites during that same time period.

To make it even more difficult for African Americans, Mississippi charged them a poll tax — a fee of $2 (equivalent to $15 in 2014) — to register, but which most whites didn't have to pay. In addition, black residents had to pass an oral literacy test administered by the county registrar, who was white and rigged it so black people were sure to fail. He often made applicants explain a certain complicated section of the state constitution or read parts of it out loud without mispronouncing any of the legalese. It was up to the registrar whether or not someone passed. The poll tax and literacy tests (which years later were ruled unconstitutional) were designed for one purpose only — to deprive African Americans, other nonwhites, and poor whites the legal right to vote.

In Leflore County, where there were almost twice as many blacks as whites, everyone knew that if black people were able to vote, the whites would lose their political clout. And there was no way the whites were going to let that happen without a fight — sometimes to the death.

To strengthen their side, SNCC joined forces with the NAACP and CORE to form the Council of Federated Organizations, or COFO, so that the groups could coordinate their efforts.

Although it was a daunting assignment, Luvaghn, Sam, Guyot, and other brave volunteers continued their door-to-door campaign to convince people to register. More often than not, fear trumped courage. The sharecroppers and farmhands were simply too dependent on their bosses — the white landowners — to make a living. Attempting to register meant almost certain loss of job and home.

Danger followed the civil rights workers. Some were beaten up; others arrested. Sam had been attacked several times and once had to jump behind a telephone pole to avoid getting run over. At night, they had to duck between houses to avoid getting snatched by roving gangs of whites. In case he was followed, Luvaghn always took a different route to the "freedom house" — a secret residence where he and other activists slept. At times when it seemed too risky to stay there, he slept at a supporter's house in the next town.

Despite the perils, Luvaghn and his comrades walked down the streets during the day, because they wanted residents to see that the civil rights workers were neither afraid nor intimidated. *The people need to know that we're putting our lives on the line to make this voter registration drive happen,* Luvaghn thought.

In the midst of all the difficulty, there were small successes. More young people were joining the struggle, and the black community increasingly embraced the activists, providing them with food and shelter. Older people began finding the courage that had been missing since the registration drive began in Greenwood.

At one voting rights meeting held in a church, Clarence Jordan, an impoverished black man who had toiled on the land for more than 40 years in Leflore County, told the audience: "I'm fightin' for my grandchildren so they won't have to go through what I'm goin' through."

Fannie Lou Hamer, who was fired from her job at a cotton plantation and evicted from her home because she attempted to register, told the crowd that someone had fired 16 bullets into the house where she was staying. "We've just got to stand up now as Negroes for ourselves and for our freedom," she said. "And if it don't do me any good, I know it will do good for the young people."

When fall arrived, the white citizens' council decided to squelch the voter registration drive by resorting to a callous, inhumane tactic — starving the poorest of the poor, who were mostly black. The late fall and winter months were always lean times, because it was the season when share-croppers and farm workers in the Mississippi Delta made little or no income. They relied on a federal program that shipped free basic food staples such as flour, rice, beans, and canned goods to various states, counties, and welfare agencies for distribution to the poverty-stricken.

In Greenwood, the vindictive white citizens' council, which controlled all local politics, ordered the Leflore County Board of Supervisors to stop doling out the free supplies on the phony excuse that the county couldn't afford to distribute them. The board did what it was told and cut off the vital food source to more than 20,000 African Americans and several thousand poor whites and Native Americans. Like his comrades, Luvaghn was outraged.

Within weeks, the food blockade had created an increasingly grave situation. COFO sent out an appeal for help to its supporters and chapters as well as to college campuses, churches, and wealthier communities throughout the country. The response was tremendous and boosted Luvaghn's faith in humanity. Black celebrities such as singer Harry Belafonte and comedian Dick Gregory raised funds and chartered planes to deliver emergency food supplies to Greenwood. College students from other states skipped classes to bring food to the besieged area. From north of the Mason-Dixon Line, white and black families and church groups packed their cars with supplies and drove hundreds of miles to deliver them.

Michigan State University students Ivanhoe Donaldson and Ben Taylor headed down in a truck loaded with food, clothing, and medicine. But racist officials were tipped off and intercepted the vehicle in Clarksdale, Mississippi, 60 miles north of Greenwood. The two students were arrested for "possession of narcotics" — which weren't drugs at all but rather aspirin and vitamins. Held on a whopping $15,000 bail (the equivalent of $118,000 in 2014), Donaldson and Taylor were kept in jail for 11 days until a nationwide protest bore enough pressure on local officials to release them. The food, clothing, and medicine, however, "mysteriously" disappeared. Ivanhoe would not be denied. Over the following months, he delivered a dozen truckloads of food to the hungry of Greenwood.

One dreary winter day, Luvaghn was passing out food and clothes to poor black people from a truck that had come from up North. He noticed that standing in the back of the line was a white family — a husband, wife, and two kids — who, judging by their threadbare clothes, looked extremely poor.

"Are we going to give *them* food?" Luvaghn asked a comrade.

"I don't know. Should we?"

The years of hostility Luvaghn harbored toward whites had initially clouded his judgment. "These supplies are for *our* people," he said. "Why should we help the whites after what they've done to Negroes?"

But as the two discussed it further, Luvaghn came to a realization: "If we want to be treated as equals, then we have to treat others as equals," he said. "These folks haven't done anything wrong. They're just like everyone else here — they need food, and their kids are hungry."

His fellow worker agreed. When the white family reached the front of the line, Luvaghn handed them a box of supplies. The humbled husband and wife thanked him and left. *It must have been extremely difficult for them to ask us Negroes for help,* Luvaghn thought.

The simple act of giving food and clothes to a needy white family changed his perspective. Up until then, he had viewed virtually all white Mississippians as the enemy — people to hate and, in many cases, people to fear. But no longer. He now understood that many whites were no different than him other than the color of their skin.

Despite months of ongoing sabotage, intimidation, and false arrests, the food blockade eventually backfired. As news reached the rest of the country that Leflore County was starving people who simply wanted to vote, Americans were horrified. The white citizens' council, which was always concerned about its image as a group of upstanding leaders of the community, was roundly condemned in the press and the pulpit.

More important, however, the blockade gave civil rights workers an opportunity to promote voter registration. Every time food was handed out to a hungry family, the activists explained reasons why people needed to register. The supplies were known as "food for those who want to be free." To get that freedom, the activists explained, you had to vote; and to vote, you had to register; and to register, you had to pass the literacy test. So COFO volunteers helped people prepare for the literacy test and escorted them to the courthouse — but still with limited success because of the fear factor.

As the civil rights workers slowly gained the black community's trust, the violence in Greenwood increased. Luvaghn's friend Jimmy Travis, who was now a SNCC worker, was severely wounded when gunmen's bullets riddled the car he was riding in. A week after the shooting, a white passenger in a passing station wagon fired a shotgun into a parked car where Sam Block and several student activists were sitting. Miraculously, no one was hurt. Days later, the Ku Klux Klan firebombed COFO's new office, destroying important records. Two nights later, a shotgun was fired into the home of a local SNCC worker. The shots blasted through the wall of a bedroom where three children slept, but they were not struck.

If the extremists thought the black residents would cower from the latest onslaught, they were wrong. Black people of all ages began marching in protest over the violence. After many were arrested, others stepped in and braved snarling police dogs and billy club–swinging cops to continue the demonstrations. Meanwhile, hundreds upon hundreds of black adults — understanding there was strength in numbers — were striding up to the courthouse seeking to register to vote even though they knew they would be denied.

Luvaghn could tell there was a growing sense of pride, commitment, and courage in the black people of Greenwood. He could see it in their eyes and in their body language, and hear it in their voices when they sang. When Luvaghn arrived in Greenwood the previous August, some residents were too scared to talk to him, too frightened to stand up for their rights. But now, more than one thousand were actively involved in the cause by marching, canvassing, attending meetings, providing food and shelter for workers, and putting up bail money.

We still have a long way to go, but we are making a difference, Luvaghn told himself. *We are changing the face of America.*

The efforts of civil rights workers like Luvaghn Brown, Lawrence Guyot, Sam Block, and others in Greenwood helped lay the groundwork for Congress to pass the Civil Rights Act in 1964 and the Voting Rights Act in 1965. Because of the historic discrimination against black people in Mississippi, the federal government monitored voter registration and elections in the state for several decades until 2014.

Worn out from his voting rights struggle in Greenwood in the early 1960s, Sam Block left his home state of Mississippi and worked in an import-export business until his death in 2000 from complications from diabetes.

In 1964, Guyot became director of the Mississippi Freedom Democratic Party. Two years later, he ran for Congress as an antiwar candidate but lost. He received a degree in law in 1971 from Rutgers University and for years spoke out on voting rights issues. Guyot worked for the Department of Human Services' Office of Early Childhood Development in Washington, DC. Suffering from heart problems, he died in 2012.

After his time in Greenwood, Luvaghn worked for SNCC in Chicago and then in New York City, where he also taught remedial reading and math in a Harlem antipoverty program. After drifting from job to job, he earned a master's degree in social welfare at State University of New York at Stony

Brook. He then worked for the accounting firm of Coopers & Lybrand and retired 28 years later as a managing director.

Living in Hartsdale, New York, Luvaghn is married with an adult daughter. He speaks to students, church groups, and civic groups and helps educate teachers about civil rights. He is involved in several civic organizations, including Facing History and Ourselves, African American Men of Westchester, and the Westchester County Domestic Violence Council.

"What happened in the 1960s was one of the most dynamic and dramatic periods in American history," he says. "I learned during that time that if you want change, you have to fight for it — and you have to be willing to make sacrifices to achieve your goals."

CAROL BARNER AND THE STOLEN GIRLS OF AMERICUS

It was a real-life nightmare that 13-year-old Carol Barner could never have imagined. Following a protest march, she and more than a dozen other girls had been shuffled from one jail to another — even though they were never formally charged with any crime.

Now here they were deep in the south Georgia woods in front of a dreary, weathered cinder-block building that looked like it had been abandoned for decades.

"Where are we?" a girl asked one of the deputies who had brought them here.

When he wouldn't respond, Carol replied, "We are somewhere in the middle of nowhere."

The deputies herded the girls through an open steel door and into a 12-foot-by-40-foot musty concrete room that reeked of urine and mildew. The barren, filthy room had no beds or any furnishings other than a pile of rotting mattresses in one corner. It was lit by a lone bare lightbulb that dangled from the cracked ceiling. The glass panes on the barred windows were broken and jagged, allowing flies, cockroaches, and mosquitoes full access to the inside. In the bathroom, the lone commode had no water in it and didn't work. Water dripped from a single broken showerhead.

"Welcome to your new home," said a deputy. "You're gonna be here a while." He gave a little chuckle and added, "A long while."

The door slammed behind them followed by a click of the rusty lock.

"What is this place?" someone asked in a voice tinged with dread.

No one knew.

"Does anyone back home know we are here?" asked another girl.

Carol chose not to blurt out a reply because the thought was too devastating. What she feared was actually the truth: To their families back home in Americus, Georgia, the girls had simply vanished — their fate unknown.

That night, curled up on the grimy floor, she thought about that spring day four months earlier that eventually led her to this horrible prison.

In March 1963, Carol, then 12, was playing outside in the yard when two college-age civil rights workers — one black and one white — walked up and began talking to her about racial inequality.

Even though half of the 13,000 residents in Americus were black, the whites had all the power and used it to make life miserable for African Americans. "We're treated lower than dirt," the young black man told Carol. "We can't sit at the lunch counters, can't use the front door at certain restaurants, can't vote."

"That's the truth," Carol said. "If a white person comes into the shop while the clerk is waiting on me, I have to step aside, or I'll get a tongue lashing. I'm not treated equally."

"Well, we aim to change that," said the white guy. "But it requires commitment and involvement, mostly on the part of students like you. There will be a meeting tonight at Allen Chapel at 6 P.M."

At the meeting, which Carol attended, members of SNCC and the NAACP explained the need for direct, nonviolent action — pickets, sit-ins, and protest marches targeting segregated establishments and stores that refused to hire or serve back people. Carol volunteered to do her part and went to training sessions in civil disobedience and passive resistance.

During one of the regular marches that challenged white supremacy in Americus, police halted Carol and her fellow marchers and ordered them to disperse. Instead, Carol and about 100 other protestors — mostly college, high school, and grade school students — sat down and sang freedom songs and prayed out loud. Offering no resistance, they were taken to the city jail and locked up without being booked or fingerprinted. They were never officially charged.

Carol wasn't scared about being behind bars. She viewed her first time in a jail cell as an exciting learning experience. It also helped that her mother, Helen, was allowed to bring her home-cooked meals — collard greens, rice and gravy, smothered fried chicken one day and pork chops, peas, and cornbread another day. A Mason jar of orange Kool-Aid accompanied each meal.

After three days in jail, Carol and the others were released. Her confinement did nothing but strengthen her resolve to continue her involvement in the movement. So on a steamy July day, Carol, who had just turned 13, was back on the front lines in another major protest march, this time targeting the segregation policies at the Martin Theater and the Trailways bus station. Most of the 300 participants were children.

As the marchers headed uptown toward the Sumter County courthouse in Americus, black supporters of all ages stood on both sides of the street in their neighborhood, clapping and cheering for them. The mood was festive, almost like a parade. Carol waved to her younger brother, Fred, who was at curbside. In response, he tossed her a few coins from his meager allowance. *I guess he thinks that if I go to jail, I might need some money to eat,* she thought, picking up the coins.

Brimming with confidence, she told herself, *If I'm arrested again, so what? If I'm beaten, so what? Maybe my sacrifice will mean my brothers and sisters will have a better life and won't have to go through the things that I've gone through.*

Some of her bravado, however, seeped out when, after reaching the crest of a hill, she saw a swarm of police clad in blue uniforms and wearing helmets with shields. Some were slapping billy clubs in their palms while others were clutching electric cattle prods. They formed an ominous human blockade. *Who are they?* Carol wondered. *I've never seen them before. Where did they come from? They look like aliens from another planet.*

Sumter County Sheriff Fred Chappell — whom Dr. Martin Luther King, Jr., once called "the meanest man in the world" after spending time in his jail — strode in front of the formidable force. Spitting out a stream of tobacco juice from the chaw lodged in one of his jowly cheeks, he signaled for the men to charge. In the past, when police confronted protestors, a warning to disperse was given first. But not this time. The helmeted police rushed into the crowd, clubbing defenseless young people, and shocking them with the cattle prods.

An officer grabbed Carol by the arm so roughly she thought it would be pulled out of her shoulder, and he dragged her toward a paddy wagon. A cop with a cattle prod rushed over. Just as the policeman was about to shock Carol, a fellow marcher, Edward Thomas, who was already in the paddy wagon, yanked her into the vehicle.

Other demonstrators weren't so lucky and were zapped or clubbed before being tossed into the paddy wagons. "They're throwing us in here like we're animals," Carol declared. "Nobody is resisting arrest, but they're hurting us, anyway."

Shoved into the paddy wagon was Carol's 13-year-old cousin LuLu Westbrook, whose face was covered with blood. "A cop attacked me with his club for no reason," moaned the dazed girl. "He was on me, beating me over the head."

Crammed into the caged vehicle, which was well beyond its capacity, the protestors were carted off to the county jail, where they spent the next three days. Carol comforted the youngest demonstrators, who were scared about their fate. By singing freedom songs and praying, the older students were able to calm the younger ones.

But the jail soon became overcrowded because the marches continued each day, and so did the arrests. Dozens of kids, including Carol and her cousins LuLu and Gloria Westbrook and Sandra Russell, were transferred to the Terrell County Jail, 30 miles away in Dawson, Georgia. African Americans called it Terrible County because of its frightening history of white-on-black violence and lynchings.

The girls and boys were separated but were on the same floor. To pass the time, the two groups took turns trying to out-sing one another. Irritated by the raucous singing, the guards ordered the kids to be quiet, but that only made the students belt out the tunes that much louder.

As punishment, the boys were shoved into the sweat box and kept there overnight. Then it was the girls' turn. Fifteen of them between the ages of 12 and 16, including Carol and her cousins, were packed into the pitch-black, stiflingly hot room. With no ventilation, the only way to get air was to lie on the concrete floor next to the door and breathe through the crack between the bottom of the door and the floor. One of the girls was afraid of the dark, and she panicked and begged to be let out. Her pleas were ignored. The next morning, when the girls were finally released from the sweat box, the walls and floors were dripping with condensation from the heat of their bodies.

The days in the county jail stretched into a week, then two, then three. Because the girls had no change of clothes and none were provided, they had to wash out their under-wear. *At least we're able to take showers,* Carol thought.

One night, after the girls had been in the Dawson jail for 3 weeks, 2 white, armed deputies told Carol's group of 15 girls they were leaving but wouldn't tell them where they were going. The girls were taken away in a prison van that had no windows in the back. At first, the girls thought that they were being returned to Americus, where they would be released.

But then the van crossed over a set of railroad tracks. Anticipation of freedom turned to a growing sense of worry. "We're not on our way home," Carol told the others. "There are no railroad tracks between Dawson and Americus."

They peppered one another with worrisome questions — ones for which they had no answers: "Where are we going?" "Why would they move us at night?" "What's going to hap-pen to us?" "Are they planning to kill us?" Now Carol was getting scared.

Less than an hour later, the van rumbled down a dirt road bordered by trees and thick brush and stopped at a clearing in front of a decaying, creepy, one-story building with barred windows. They were put inside a stinking, grimy concrete room and told this would be their new prison. It had no beds, no running water, no working toilet.

The stunned kids stared at their disgusting surround-ings, not knowing what to say. They were devastated and overwhelmed not only by their situation but by the stench, filth, insects, and heat. No one wanted to sit down or touch anything. The only things even remotely useable were some smelly, stained army blankets full of cigarette burns.

To quench their thirst, they took turns standing under the rusty, dripping showerhead and cupped their hands to catch drops of warm water. *There's no place to sleep or take a bath or go to the bathroom,* Carol told herself. "We've never been charged with any crime, yet we're treated like criminals," she said out loud. "No, actually, we're treated worse than criminals. At least they get a bed and a shower and a toilet."

"What are we going to do?" asked a girl, her voice beginning to crack.

"You can either sleep standing up or on this dirty floor," replied Carol as she pressed her back against a wall and slid into a sitting position. By now the youngest kids began whimpering and a few began wailing. Carol wanted to cry, too, but she didn't. *I have to be strong for the others,* she told herself. She consoled one of the younger ones, who put her head on Carol's shoulder.

Their guard was an overweight elderly man in bib overalls who carried a shotgun and lived in an office at the front of the decrepit prison. He wasn't mean like the deputies, but did little to help the girls other than give them three tin cups to collect water from the dripping showerhead.

The next day, the girls asked the old man — whose name was Mr. Countryman, but they called him Pops — for a broom so they could sweep up the room. He obliged them and explained that they were being held prisoner in a condemned stockade that had been built and used during the Civil War. The stockade was near Leesburg, Georgia, about 25 miles south of Americus.

Later that afternoon, Mr. Story, Americus's white dogcatcher, arrived with boxes of cold hamburgers for the girls — their first food in more than 24 hours. Every day, he delivered them much the same awful rations — hamburgers that were charred on the edges and raw on the inside or runny egg salad sandwiches that were made with mayonnaise that had often turned rancid. Carol was savvy enough to nibble on the burnt part of the burgers and avoid the undercooked middle. She stayed away from the egg salad. Many of the girls who ate the revolting sandwiches got sick from food poisoning and were throwing up or suffering from diarrhea.

Everyone was losing weight and many were sick from ear infections, boils, high fevers, and infected insect bites. LuLu desperately needed medical treatment for her untreated head wound.

Without soap, toothpaste, or running water, the girls smelled bad. They had to urinate over the shower drain and defecate in used cardboard hamburger containers. They wiped themselves with the paper that the burgers were wrapped in.

The oppressive heat, disgusting odor, and creepy crawlies combined to magnify the girls' misery. *This place isn't fit for humans or even animals,* Carol thought. Throughout the day and especially at night, different girls would break down and weep from living in such horrific conditions. Whenever someone felt she could no longer cope, others would hug her and give her words of encouragement even if they didn't believe the sentiments themselves.

The original 15 girls were soon joined by another 18 who also had been arrested for demonstrating against racial injustice. To maintain their sanity, they tried different activities. Because they were all church-going children of faith, they conducted group prayers every day. Some of the girls preached and reminded the others, "God will take care of us."

They sang freedom songs as well as Top 40 tunes. They occasionally put on talent shows — mostly singing and dancing — and acted out scenes from movies and tried to make one another laugh. Sometimes they talked about their hopes and dreams after they got out of this repulsive modern-day dungeon — if they got out. They tried not to think that "maybe today is the day we go home" because that only led to disappointment when night came and they were still imprisoned. At times, they shared what they missed most about home. Carol said she missed her six siblings and her mom's cooking. What preyed on the girls' minds daily was worrying about their families and how distraught they must be, not knowing the kids' whereabouts or whether they were dead or alive.

Carol's 12-year-old cousin Sandra Russell confided that she feared they would never see their home again. "I really feel in my heart like they're planning on killing us, and nobody will ever know what happened to us," she said.

Because Sandra was so petite and looked much younger than her age, Pops felt sorry for her and often had her sit and talk with him in his office. Sometimes he shared food that he cooked on an electric hot plate. She would eat half of her portion and bring the rest back to the room to give to someone else.

During an early visit, Sandra had a chance to talk to Mr. Story, the dogcatcher. "Your people need to know you are here," he told her. After she gave him the names of the girls and their parents, he promised to get word to the families who had been frantically making the rounds of area jails, trying to find their abducted children.

He stayed true to his word and secretly contacted the parents, who then gave him food to bring back to the young prisoners. Hardly any of the parents had a car, so everyone was grateful to Mr. Story. They knew that if he were caught by the police — a white person smuggling in food to black kids — he likely would be beaten or killed.

Occasionally, some parents who had a car and enough money for a bribe were able to take their daughters home.

One day, Carol's, Sandra's, and Emmarene Kaigler's mothers borrowed a car and showed up at the stockade unexpectedly, bearing clothes, food, and soap for their daughters. The reunion, held through the barred windows, triggered tears of joy from the mothers who finally had proof that their kids were alive.

"How are you doing?" Carol's mother, Helen, asked her.

"I'm okay, Mama."

"Do you want to get out?"

"Sure. But will it cost money?"

"Yes. That's how some of the girls managed to get freed and are back home now. I can borrow the money."

Although she yearned to go home, Carol shook her head and said, "I didn't pay to get in and I won't pay to get out. Besides, Mama, you'd be paying interest for a long time and never get ahead. And there's another reason why I have to stay here. Most of the families can't afford to get their kids out of here, and I don't want to leave them."

Carol could tell her mother wanted to burst out crying but managed to stifle herself. "I don't know if I'll ever get another chance to get back here," Helen said.

"Don't worry, Mama. I'll be all right. Someday we'll be together again."

Compounding their despair, the girls sometimes felt threatened. Occasionally, Pops was given a break and replaced by guards who enjoyed taunting the girls. Some guards poked the girls with sticks and called them "picka-ninnies," "jungle bunnies," and "niggers." One guard lied to them that Dr. King had been locked up for good. "Who's gonna be your savior now?" he sneered. (In fact, Dr. King was in Washington, DC, at the time, giving his famous "I Have a Dream" speech in front of 250,000 people.)

To terrorize the girls, a guard once tossed a live snake into the room. The girls shrieked in horror and cowered in the opposite corner, only moving when the squirming reptile came near them. Finally, the door opened and in walked a tall, slim stranger with a big hat and fancy boots. He strode over to the snake from behind and with catlike swiftness picked it up behind its head and tossed it out the window.

Seeing the open door, the screeching girls dashed out of the stockade and scampered across the clearing toward the woods. But then they didn't know which way to go.

Pops got his shotgun and was shouting at them to stop. Carol yelled to the girls, "No! No! No! If we run into the woods, we'll get lost and all sorts of bad things could hap-pen to us. Animals could get us. Even if that doesn't happen, we're black girls who escaped from a prison. If we're caught, we'll be killed. Come on, let's go back. We're safer inside than we are outside."

Reluctantly, the girls agreed. They turned around and trudged solemnly into the stockade. Pops, who would have been severely punished if they had escaped, was relieved they hadn't. "We're all accounted for," Carol told him. "We're all here."

Not long afterward, two pickups full of white teenage boys guzzling bottles of beer roared up to the stockade. They shouted to Pops, "Let us in with those nigger girls so we can have a little fun!"

Looking out through the barred windows, the girls were petrified. "Those rednecks want to kill us," Carol said.

Pops fired his shotgun in the air. "Get away from here and don't ever come back!" he thundered. Then to make his point absolutely clear, he fired the shotgun again. The trucks rooster-tailed out of sight.

Weeks dragged on for the girls — three, four, five weeks. Although some lucky girls had managed to buy their freedom, the original 15 girls still remained captive.

One day in late August, they heard a car drive up. A young black man got out of a Volkswagen and started a conversation with Pops. As the girls peered through the windows, they were startled to see the trunk open and a young white man with a camera emerge. While the driver was diverting Pops's attention, the photographer scurried around the corner of the stockade to a window in the back.

"Are you a freedom fighter?" Carol whispered to him.

He flashed a peace sign and nodded. "I'm Danny Lyon," he answered in a low voice. "SNCC sent me to take photos of you girls to prove that you're being held here illegally and under inhumane conditions. I don't have much time."

He explained to them the kind of photos he wanted, so they showed him how they slept on the floor and what they did to pass the time. They pointed out the unsanitary conditions of the squalid prison, and they modeled their soiled, torn clothes for him.

As they gathered for a group picture, Sandra told Carol, "I'm gonna put my hand on my hip and smile because when Mama sees this, she'll know I'm okay."

Everyone smiled. Instead of saying *cheese*, they said *freedom* — but quietly because they didn't want to alert Pops, who was still talking to Lyon's driver. After he had taken the pictures he needed, Lyon thanked the girls and told them, "You are all so beautiful."

He sneaked back into the trunk of the car. Then the driver said good-bye to the unsuspecting Pops and drove off. Lyon had to hide in the trunk because for a white guy to be seen riding with a black man could cause them physical harm — or worse.

Several days later, the paddy wagon showed up and two deputies ordered the girls to get in without telling them where they were going. Some assumed they were being transferred to another jail, which was all right with them because anything was better than the run-down stockade. Others fretted that they might be slain.

But their mood soared when they arrived at the Sumter County Jail in Americus. There, waiting for them, where their teary-eyed parents. After 45 days of captivity in the stockade, the girls were finally freed. They learned that

Lyon, a 21-year-old New Yorker who worked for SNCC in Atlanta, had their photos published in several publications, which referred to the kids as the Stolen Girls. The publicity over their plight led directly to their release.

However, a few of the girls, including Carol, still had to face a judge. In the courtroom, the judge asked her, "Do you intend to get involved in this mess again?"

Her weeks as a Stolen Girl did nothing to quell her spirit. Angered by his question, Carol stared the judge in the eye and, in a voice rising with every word, replied, "What mess? I was in a peaceful civil rights demonstration for equal rights. If the next mess, as you call it, is another peaceful civil rights demonstration, I'll be the first in line."

The more she spoke, the angrier she became, ignoring her mother Helen's frantic attempts to shut her up.

"If you get involved in this mess again, I'm going to send you to a reform school," the judge warned.

Carol shot back, "I have been locked up for three days in the county jail, three weeks in Dawson, and forty-five days in the middle of nowhere sleeping on a filthy concrete floor. And you're threatening me about reform school? At least they will feed me decent food and give me a bed to sleep in. So if you want to lock me away in a reform school, do me a favor and lock me up now and throw away the key."

Helen was crying, certain that the judge was going to ship Carol off. "Please, Carol, don't talk that way. I beg you."

Carol snapped, "Mama, be quiet. Why are you crying in front of this white man?"

"See?" the judge said to Helen. "This girl of yours is

disrespectful to you and to me. She won't even address me as 'Your Honor' or 'sir.' My children would never talk to an adult the way she does."

"I'm not being disrespectful," Carol countered. "You are."

"Hush, Carol, hush," Helen pleaded. "You're only digging yourself deeper in trouble."

Carol brushed off her mother's caution and told the judge, "Would your white children say 'yes, ma'am' and 'no, ma'am' to my black mama?"

The judge's face turned red from exasperation. Then he bellowed to Helen, "Get her out of here!"

The time in captivity had drastically changed Carol. Her childhood had been stripped of innocence. Her days of playing with dolls and jacks and jumping rope were over, and she no longer could go back to being a little girl anymore. Her experience had made her tougher, stronger, and wiser — more grown-up and less childlike.

Carol and the other Stolen Girls had missed two weeks of school by the time they were released. When they returned to their classrooms, they discovered it wouldn't be easy for them to fit in. Rather than being treated as heroines, they were ridiculed by fellow students as criminals. Typical of what they faced: One classmate would loudly ask, "What kind of bird doesn't fly?" Other classmates would shout in unison, "A jailbird!"

When one of the Stolen Girls complained about the teasing, Carol told her, "Don't let it bother you. They're ignorant. Those kids just don't understand that what we did — marching and protesting and sacrificing — wasn't for us, it was for everyone. We paid a heavy price. We suffered for a cause we believed in. And I'm still committed to that cause. If I have to do it all over again, I'll do it all over again."

Carol and her cousin Sandra Russell were actively involved in the civil rights movement throughout the rest of their school years. Upon graduation, Carol left town, married, and raised a son. After getting her doctorate at Andersonville Theological Seminary, she became a pastor in Americus. Now affiliated with Holy Life Ministries International, Apostle Dr. Carol Barner Seay trains pastors and helps start new churches.

Carol and Sandra (whose married name was Mansfield) were inducted into the National Voting Rights Museum Hall of Fame in Selma, Alabama, in 2007. Sandra, the mother of four and grandmother of eight, died in 2012.

In 2003, on the fortieth anniversary of their imprisonment, a documentary called LuLu and the Girls of Americus, Georgia, 1963 *premiered in Americus to critical acclaim.*

Although the Stolen Girls all took various paths in life, they share a bond forever marked by their unconscionable police abduction and captivity in the summer of 1963. Some of them have reported that they still suffer recurring nightmares or have sought counseling. Many others, like Carol, refused for years to talk about their time in the stockade, even with their spouses and children. In fact, Carol and Sandra never discussed it with each other despite being together often.

"I buried the memory of it for thirty-three years so deeply I didn't even remember it," Carol says. In 1996, at a local

gathering, she and her cousins Gloria and LuLu Westbrook were asked to share their recollections about their days in the civil rights movement. "We started sharing, and it hurt so badly that we couldn't finish the story," Carol recalls. "There was so much crying I ran out of the room. The tears that never were when I was locked up suddenly came flooding out. But I didn't talk about it again for another eight years.

"Now I talk about it all the time at colleges, churches, senior citizens' groups, and other organizations because I want people to understand there was a price to pay for our freedom. America was supposed to be the land of the free, but it really wasn't for black people in the South. We had to fight for the freedoms we enjoy today."

FRANK BATES AND THE CRAWFORDVILLE PROTESTS

Sixteen-year-old Frank Bates lay facedown on the pavement directly in front of a full school bus and dared the startled driver to run over him. It was Frank's desperate attempt to stop the bus from transporting white students to an all-white school that refused to admit black kids like him. He wanted to dramatize the injustice that had been inflicted on him and his fellow students even at the risk of his own life.

For months, Frank had helped lead student protests, boycotts, and marches seeking school integration and racial equality. But little had changed in the deeply segregated town of Crawfordville, Georgia. In fact, it had turned worse.

He and many others had been arrested and jailed and threatened; some had even been badly beaten up. But he never wavered in his dedication to the cause.

And now Frank Bates was prepared to die. And so were

several other black students who followed his lead and sprawled, one next to the other, on the street.

He was lying about three feet from the front tires of the bus when a white supremacist ran up to the vehicle and thundered to the driver, "Get out of there! Let me drive the bus! I'll run over them damn niggers!"

White onlookers began cheering him while others jeered the silently protesting African Americans on the pavement. Suddenly, fear began to sweep over Frank. He knew that this local man was crazy enough to run over him and the other demonstrators. The man jumped into the bus, pulled the driver off the seat, and plopped down behind the wheel. Then he gunned the engine.

Frank's heart pounded; his muscles tightened. As the engine whined, the driver eased off the clutch, and the bus inched forward. *Don't get up,* Frank thought. *Stay put. He wouldn't really run us over, would he?*

The man raced the engine and once again let up on the clutch. The bus crept closer to Frank's prone body. *Stay strong!* As the bus kept inching forward, Frank could hear the subtle crunch of tiny stones getting squashed on the slowly rotating tires. *Don't get up!* The bus edged closer and closer . . .

The youngest of seven children, Frank grew up in Level Hill, a tiny black farming community near Crawfordville about 100 miles east of Atlanta.

He lived and worked on his family's 257-acre farm — one of the few farms in the area owned by a black man. Work was important for the Bates kids because their daddy and granddaddy believed in living by the sweat of your brow.

Like his parents and siblings before him, Frank attended all-black Level Hill Elementary — a ramshackle one-room schoolhouse. From first through fourth grade, students sat on hard wooden benches around an eight-foot table. By fifth grade, the kids graduated to chairs. Unlike his parents who never got beyond the fourth grade because they had to work the farm, Frank continued his all-black education at Murden Elementary and Murden High School in Crawfordville.

Murden was no different than most black schools in the South. It lacked all the nice things that were in the nearby all-white county high school, Alexander H. Stephens Institute, such as a gym, an auditorium, and updated textbooks. Frank and his teammates on the school basketball squad had to play their games outside on hard clay. In the 1964–65 school term, Stephens didn't have a basketball team because of a lack of interest. So the Murden team asked Taliaferro County School Superintendent Lola Williams if they could play their home games at the Stephens gym. After all, the gym was paid for by county taxpayers — both black and white. Williams, who was white, refused for no other reason than black kids weren't allowed to play in a white gym. As a consolation, she had Murden's clay basketball court asphalted.

At the end of the school term, when Frank was completing his junior year, he immersed himself in the civil rights movement. He was inspired by his science teacher and basketball coach, Calvin Turner. As head of the local voters' league,

Turner was the first black man in Crawfordville to openly challenge the white power structure in the county by encouraging African Americans to register to vote. With support and training from the SCLC, Turner became a thorn in the side of segregationists.

After the passage of the 1964 Civil Rights Act, Taliaferro (pronounced "Tolliver") County was forced to comply with federal laws requiring school integration. Encouraged by Turner and Murden High's black principal Evans Harris, Frank and 87 of his classmates signed up in spring 1965 to attend Stephens beginning in the fall.

Aghast that their children's lily-white school would become one-third black, the segregationists in town fought back. Near the end of the 1964–65 term, the school board announced it was firing Harris, Turner, and six other teachers for "causing trouble in the community" and "registering blacks to vote instead of teaching them to read and write."

Frank and his fellow students were incensed. They walked out of school and marched one mile along Lexington Avenue to Friendship Baptist Church. Then, with members of the SCLC, they continued their march to the county courthouse, demanding that the educators' contracts be renewed. School board officials refused to even meet with the demonstrators.

Soon, the protests expanded beyond the teacher firings and took aim at seeking equal rights in all facets of life in Taliaferro County. With Frank leading the way, the students targeted Bonner's Café — a restaurant that required African Americans to enter from the back and whites from the front. Frank and several of his classmates walked into the front and asked to be served. The owner refused, so they sat down on the front steps until the police arrived and took them to the station, where they were scolded and released.

To get around the law, the owner of Bonner's Café turned it into a "members-only" establishment. Frank and his friends filled out membership applications and submitted them. To no one's surprise, the applications were rejected.

When several black students tried to use the whites-only coin laundry, they were arrested. Black activists then began a boycott of all the white businesses in Crawfordville and picketed in front of the stores.

As summer heated up, Frank organized a swim-in where black kids planned to jump into the all-white pool at A. H. Stephens State Park (named after the vice president of the Confederacy during the Civil War). On the day of the swim-in, Frank heard rumors that the whites had poisoned the pool with potash and lye meant to burn the skin. Despite fears they would be harmed, he and his fellow protestors chose to go ahead with their demonstration and paid their admission. Already alerted to the swim-in, the white kids stayed out of the pool while the black kids milled around the pool deck.

No one wanted to test the waters. "Well, Frank, you've been our leader," said a fellow student. "So go ahead and lead."

With some apprehension, Frank jumped into the pool. The good news was the water hadn't been tainted. The bad news was that Frank couldn't swim. While he was thrashing about, trying to keep his head above water, the others thought he was playing around so they jumped in, too.

Frank went into panic mode, flogging, gagging, and desperately trying to keep from drowning. He struggled so hard that he dislocated his shoulder. Realizing that Frank was in trouble, his friend Robert Revere came to the rescue and pulled him out of the pool. Frank was in so much pain that Calvin Turner drove him to the hospital in nearby Greensboro 20 miles away. "Well, at least it was a great day for everybody else," Frank told Turner. "We desegregated the pool."

As Frank continued to lead student demonstrations for equality, white thugs began physically attacking SCLC volunteers, both white and black college students from throughout the country who had come to town to help speed voter registration and integration in Crawfordville. They were constantly facing harassment and death threats. For intimidation, the KKK set a cross on fire in an open field near town and demanded that black residents stop boycotting white businesses.

Frank and his fellow activists didn't back down. He continued to help organize and lead Sunday protest marches, pickets, and mass meetings, which were starting to get media attention. To make it look like Crawfordville wasn't racist, the town hired a 66-year-old retired sawmill operator, Jesse Meadows, as their police chief, making him the first African American to hold such a position in the South. Never mind that he was totally unqualified, having no formal education and no law-enforcement experience other than being arrested for moonshining years earlier.

On July 16, 1965, during a demonstration, Frank was at the front of a picket line when Meadows strode up behind him and ordered, "Turn around." When Frank refused, Meadows announced, "Then you are under arrest."

"What for?"

"Disobeying a police officer." Meadows then made the first arrest of his life, putting the handcuffs on Frank and taking him to the sheriff's office. During the booking process, Meadows didn't know how to take off the handcuffs, so a sheriff's deputy had to do it. Frank spent the night in a jail cell. *They think that if they put me in jail, they will stop all the others from protesting*, he thought. *This will only make people angrier.*

Just as he thought, the sham arrest infuriated the black community. About 250 protestors — including some from Atlanta and others who had never taken part in a demonstration before — marched to the courthouse to rally on behalf of the jailed young leader. But then more than 30 African Americans, including his brother Fred, were arrested on charges of disturbing the peace. However, later that afternoon, they, along with Frank, were released. Meanwhile, Meadows's family convinced him to resign.

For Frank's mentor, Calvin Turner, life nose-dived. He was indicted on trumped-up felony charges, including one for forging black students' applications to attend Stephens Institute. He was tossed in jail under an incredibly hefty $15,000 bail (equivalent to more than $113,000 in 2014).

Meanwhile, pressure mounted against students who had signed up for Stephens. In several cases, their parents were fired from their jobs, families were evicted from their rental homes, tenant farmers were kicked off the land they tilled, and others lost their cars or homes when the banks demanded full payment on their loans. The sole reason for these despicable acts was retaliation for teenagers simply wanting to lawfully integrate a high school. Frank was proud that most of his victimized classmates didn't back out of their commitment to attend Stephens.

Marches continued throughout the summer. Frank helped lead more than 300 African Americans on August 22 from Friendship Baptist Church to the courthouse square, where they held a brief rally, prayed for justice, and sang "God Bless America." His grandfather James, Sr., was by his side. During the demonstration, Frank noticed that across the grassy square, a white jackleg preacher (an amateur clergyman who had no official training or status) was playing religious music on a windup record player and ranting against sinners. Frank didn't give him much thought.

But the next day, sheriff's deputies served warrants to Frank and his grandfather as well as Evans Harris, Calvin Turner, and Turner's father and grandfather and three others. District Attorney Kenneth Goolsby charged them with the crime of "disturbing divine worship," claiming their demonstration disrupted the self-proclaimed preacher's public sermon. It was Goolsby who had approved most of the previous questionable arrests of black protestors. The defendants bonded out, and Frank continued his civil rights efforts.

The weekly demonstrations grew even larger as the start of the fall term approached. Frank and his fellow students were excited and nervous about integrating Stephens

Institute and weren't sure what to expect. When they showed up for the first day of classes, they faced a surprise that stunned them.

The school board had secretly transferred admission of every white student and teacher to segregated schools in the surrounding counties of Warren, Wilkes, and Greene. So when the black students arrived at Stephens, they saw the white students getting onto buses bound for the neighboring counties. State troopers were overseeing the boarding while a large crowd of white parents looked on.

Once Frank got over the shock, he shouted to the black students, "Let's get on the buses, too!"

He charged toward the nearest school bus, but was tackled by an officer. Other black students tried to get on buses but the police blocked their way. "You're not going to ride the buses, and that's it!" thundered a police captain.

Frank knew he had to do something to stop the buses, or at least dramatize the unfairness of it all. Thinking fast, he wheeled around and shouted to his fellow black students, "If we can't get on the buses, then we should block them!"

Without a moment's hesitation — and without worrying about the possible consequences — he ran in front of the first bus and lay down face-first in the street. Because he was their leader, several others joined him, lining up in a row on the pavement.

As he stretched out about three feet from the big bus tires, the reality of the risk he now faced suddenly struck him. *That white bus driver just might want to run over all of us,* he thought. *We'd be crushed to death. If it means I must die, so be it. I'm not leaving.* The engine was idling but the bus didn't move. Frank felt a little less tense. *It sounds like the driver doesn't want to hurt anyone.*

But when a local racist commandeered the bus, gunned the engine, and let the bus inch forward, Frank wondered if he and his prone protestors were doomed.

Before the bus moved any closer to him, however, state troopers rushed on board and yanked the man out of the driver's seat. Seconds later, officers grabbed Frank by both arms and pulled him away from the bus. As he was being pulled to his feet, he saw that the other black students in the human blockade were also being dragged off.

From the side of the road, he watched helplessly while the filled-up buses of white students drove away to the other schools.

Any hopes that the black students could at least attend Stephens Institute were dashed when the local school board announced that it had closed the school. Officials in the school districts in the other counties claimed they couldn't take any black students from Taliaferro County because their schools were overcrowded. That meant the only school available to African Americans was Murden High.

"That's totally unacceptable," Frank told his fellow students. "We're not going back to Murden. We're not returning to a school that's missing our principal and some of our best teachers. If we can't go to a white school, we aren't going to *any* school."

The student strike spread to all grades at Murden High and Murden Elementary, so that most of the African American kids stayed away.

During the following days, black students of all ages, including some as young as seven, arrived early at Stephens Institute and tried to board the buses meant for white students. But every attempt was thwarted by the police while hostile white parents and members of the KKK cheered the cops and shouted racial insults at the African Americans.

"If they won't let us on the buses, then we're going to have to drive to the schools ourselves," Frank said. The protesting students split into three groups and headed off to the various out-of-county schools.

Frank borrowed his brother Fred's Chevrolet and, accompanied by four classmates, led a procession of several cars to the high school in Warrenton. When they neared the school, their cars were pelted with eggs and rotten apples. Frank slowed to a crawl but kept driving toward the entrance of the school, which was ringed by state police. Whites on both sides of the street were booing, taunting, and heckling the black students.

Suddenly, an enraged white man — later identified as Calvin Craig, the grand dragon of the local KKK — rushed up to Frank's slow-moving car, whipped open the door, grabbed Frank, and pulled him out onto the pavement.

When Frank hit the ground, several whites pounced on him and pummeled him. He tried to defend himself as best he could, but it was futile. Fortunately for him, the state troopers believed in some sense of law and order — unlike in other regions of the South — and quickly ended the beating. They even took a gun away from one of the assailants. Frank, whose shirt was torn off his back, was bruised and bleeding and had a black eye, but otherwise wasn't seriously hurt.

The police walked him to his Chevy, which, because it had still been in gear when he was dragged out, had rolled into a parked car, causing minor damage. However, the windshield of his car was cracked from a well-thrown rock or apple.

"I'm ordering you and your buddies to get in your cars and go back to your own county," a no-nonsense officer told Frank. "We don't need your kind causing trouble in Warrenton. You don't belong here, and we don't want you here." Police then escorted them back to Crawfordville.

With their children boycotting school and their leaders facing criminal charges, members of Taliaferro County's black community sought help from the SCLC. The group sent extra workers to help organize new protests and to set up a special "Freedom School" for 300 striking students. Volunteer teachers from around the state were recruited by the SCLC to hold classes in the Springfield community a few miles from Crawfordville.

Every morning was pretty much the same: As whites boarded school buses outside Stephens Institute, black teenagers across the street sang freedom songs and chanted, "Freedom now!"

Several times, the black students piled into cars and followed the buses to the other counties, where they tried to enter the schools. They were always turned away.

Despite his beating in Warrenton, Frank returned to the high school grounds to no avail. A film crew captured a verbal exchange between Frank and a patrolman after the cop asked him why he kept coming back.

"My friends and I are here to register at Warrenton High School," Frank explained.

"You can't register for classes today for the same reasons you couldn't register yesterday and all the days before," the officer said. "The school is full and the deadline for registering was more than a month ago."

"We didn't know our school board was going behind our backs to avoid complying with the Civil Rights Act."

"Look, you and your fellow students need to return to your cars and go home. You're asking for big trouble just by showing up here."

"But why should we have to attend a segregated school and get a second-class education?"

"You need to take up that issue with the courts." Seeing grim-faced whites beginning to assemble and walk toward the group, the officer told Frank, "Trouble is brewing. I intend to keep law and order here in Warren County this morning. And the best way to do that is for y'all to leave right now."

Frank and the others left and headed for the Springfield Freedom School. On the way back, he noticed that a state trooper was tailing him, so he was extra careful while driving. It didn't matter. The cop pulled him over and ticketed him for failing to use his turn signal even though he had used it.

As the number and intensity of the protests increased, Dr. Martin Luther King, Jr., and his wife, Coretta, came to Crawfordville on October 11. At that night's mass meeting, King addressed an overflow crowd of 700 in Friendship Baptist Church. In a resounding speech that left Frank inspired, King said, "We assemble here tonight to say to our white brothers of Georgia that there will be neither peace nor tranquillity in this community until the Negro receives justice in Crawfordville. We are determined to be free, and we are determined to achieve that freedom *now*!"

Three days later, a SCLC attorney spoke at a mass meeting at the church after receiving word of several federal court decisions that had a major impact on every local student. First, the lawyer announced that the court had dismissed charges against Frank, Calvin Turner, and the others for "disturbing divine worship" and also the forgery charges against Turner.

But the news got better, much better. The same court ruled that Taliaferro County's busing of white students to segregated schools in neighboring counties was illegal. It also placed control of the Taliaferro school system in the hands of a court-appointed trustee. Best of all, the court demanded that the schools in the three counties that had accepted the white Taliaferro County students had to enroll all 88 black students who had originally applied to Stephens Institute. School buses transporting Taliaferro County students to the other schools were now required to carry all students regardless of race.

"What makes this so sweet," said the attorney, "is that the schools that had conspired with Taliaferro County to keep classes segregated are themselves desegregated by court order."

People in the church erupted in jubilation. Frank was beside himself with joy. "We won a major victory!" he shouted. "We accomplished what we had set out to do — achieve school integration!"

*   *   *

Frank Bates and five female students were assigned to Washington High School in Wilkes County. On the first day of school, Frank was given the silent treatment by the white students. The next day, he was taken off the school bus by the sheriff and arrested for writing a bad check — a charge that was later proved false and designed solely to discredit Frank as a black leader. He spent the night in jail before he was bonded out.

On Frank's third day in school, a student cold-cocked him in the jaw. Instead of punishing the attacker, the principal suspended Frank, claiming that it was against school policy for any student to attend class while out of jail on bond.

Frank decided to complete his senior year at Murden High, but county school superintendent Lola Williams barred him because he was labeled a troublemaker. At his grandfather's insistence, Frank moved in with his brother Fred in Atlanta, where he worked during the day and went to school at night, graduating in May 1966.

The next school year (1966–67) Stephens Institute reopened as a completely integrated elementary school, and Murden was turned into an integrated high school. But many of Crawfordville's white students transferred to all-white "private academies," leaving the public schools overwhelmingly black.

Meanwhile, Williams refused to rehire the Murden High teachers that she had fired after the 1964–65 school year. Most left Crawfordville, but Calvin Turner stayed in the area, where he remained an activist and became a successful businessman and builder of affordable housing. He died in 2007 at the age of 75.

Frank attended college, served briefly in the United States Army, and eventually earned a law degree from Atlanta Law School.

Twelve years after his last arrest as a student leader, Frank phoned one of his former tormentors to make peace. He set up a meeting with Kenneth Goolsby, the prosecutor who had repeatedly put him and other demonstrators behind bars. When they met face-to-face, Goolsby told him, "I'm ready to bury the hatchet if you are." Frank replied, "Mr. Goolsby, I still stand for the same principles I stood for back in 1965. But I know a different way of going about getting change — by using the law."

Impressed by the young man who was once his nemesis, Goolsby hired Frank to handle the region's delinquent child-support cases. The former adversaries ended up becoming close friends. After six years on the job, Frank left to work as an investigator in the Georgia Office of Fair Employment Practice and then became deputy director of the Democratic Party of Georgia. He eventually worked for a state agency that dealt with drugs in the workplace before being executive assistant of community relations for Governor Zell Miller. Frank retired in 2008 and now enjoys traveling throughout the country. He is writing a book about his life, From Level Hill to Capitol Hill.

CHUCK BONNER AND BLOODY SUNDAY

Eight-year-old Charles "Chuck" Bonner was toiling in the cotton fields in Crumptonia, a remote settlement of peasant sharecroppers southwest of Selma, Alabama. Battling the sweltering heat and the razor-sharp dried bristles, he and black workers of all ages, including his young female cousin Bay Love, had been picking cotton since sunup. Chuck was tired and cranky.

As little Chuck dragged his large patched-up cotton sack along another seemingly endless row in a sea of white that Saturday, he told Bay Love that he didn't believe what their teacher had said earlier about Abraham Lincoln freeing the slaves.

"Look at all these Negroes with their long cotton sacks," Chuck said, pointing to the dozens of sweaty, bent-over workers around them. "This is what people were doin' when they were slaves one hundred years ago. How's it any different now?"

"The happiest part of the day is gettin' to the end of a row," Bay Love said.

"Something ain't right. This still looks like slavery. How is this ever gonna change?"

Bay Love didn't have the answer. Neither did Chuck.

He couldn't understand why white people looked and acted superior to black people. He couldn't understand why he lived in a weather-beaten house with no indoor plumbing while the whites slept in nice homes with electricity and flushing toilets. He couldn't understand why he and his friends attended a little one-room school with a black potbelly stove in back of Athens Baptist Church while the white kids went to a new brick schoolhouse with a manicured lawn. Many nights during his bedside prayers, he asked God, "Why the big difference? I thought we were all God's children, because that's what I was taught in Sunday school."

In 1958, when he was 11, Chuck settled in with his mother and stepfather in Selma, the seat of Dallas County and the economic, political, and cultural center of western Alabama. The county was controlled with an iron fist by Sheriff Jim Clark, Judge James Hare, and the powerful white citizens' council. More than 80 percent of the black adults in the county lived below the poverty line, working mostly as sharecroppers, farmhands, maids, janitors, and day laborers. Only 5 percent had a high school diploma, mostly because the state made little effort to provide educational opportunities for black people.

In the only world he knew, African Americans were simply second-class citizens. He didn't like it, but what choice did he have?

One winter Sunday in 1963, Chuck and his friend Cleophus Hobbs, both 16, were in the street, pushing the Bonners' green 1954 Ford, which had broken down. A young black man in his early 20s, dressed in a yellow button-down shirt, tie, and sports jacket, walked up to the boys and helped them shove the car to the Bonner residence.

On the way, he introduced himself as Bernard Lafayette, Jr., who had just moved to Selma from Tennessee with his young bride, Colia. He said he was from the Student Nonviolent Coordinating Committee. Bernard explained that he had moved to Selma to organize students in a voter-registration drive and in direct action to integrate the area's lunch counters, libraries, movie theaters, schools, and restaurants.

"Students are the ones who'll have to bear the brunt of the movement here," he told them. "Undoubtedly they will be arrested and beaten and spat on. Some might even get killed. But I'd like you to join me. I will teach you to succeed through nonviolence and how to protect yourselves through-out this ordeal."

"Hold on," said Chuck. "When you mean nonviolence . . ."

"I mean you do not fight back if you are hit."

Chuck and Cleo looked at each other and shook their heads. The idea of getting struck and not retaliating with your fists was unthinkable to them. You always slugged it out when there was a disagreement. That was just a given where they grew up.

"I know you have a problem with this," Bernard said. "Have you ever heard of Mahatma Gandhi?" The boys nod-ded. "Do you know the man who killed Gandhi?" They shook their heads. "You know Jesus. But do you know the names of the men who killed him?" They shook their heads. "Gandhi and Jesus were men of peace with a lasting legacy, but their killers have faded from history. Through nonviolence, Jesus and Gandhi started world movements — and that's what we want to do in Selma."

After further discussions, Chuck agreed that Bernard had made a compelling argument. Over the next several days, Chuck and Cleo began recruiting fellow students from the all-black R. B. Hudson High. Among the first to join them were their friends Terry Shaw and Bettie Mae Fikes. They soon had rounded up dozens of students who met in secret at the Tabernacle Baptist Church with Bernard and Colia.

For several months, the students studied the principles of nonviolence, learned freedom songs, and trained in tactics for direct action. Chuck and Cleo even formed their own high school version of SNCC.

In early June 1963, they distributed flyers to adults about a mass meeting at the church to discuss voter registration and the launch of Selma's freedom movement. But a cloud of fear hovered over the black community that whites would punish those who attended the meeting. Going door-to-door, Chuck and his fellow students stressed to the adults that voting was a powerful tool that could change life for the better.

The night of the meeting, the church was surrounded by Sheriff Clark and his deputies, who jotted down license numbers and took photographs of people as they entered the church. For further intimidation, Clark had brought along his posse men — white supremacists who wore khaki uniforms, construction helmets, and plastic badges and carried pistols and wooden clubs. Although hundreds of African Americans turned back rather than walk past the racists, more than 350 courageous men, women, and children attended the mass meeting — a first of its kind in Selma.

Shortly after it started, Clark, accompanied by several deputies, stormed into the church, waving a court order from Judge Hare, demanding that the meeting end immediately "to prevent insurrection." Refusing to kowtow to him, the people booed the sheriff and carried on. Speakers discussed the need to organize, challenge Jim Crow laws, and register to vote, and Bettie Mae led everyone in singing freedom songs. By the end of the evening, most in the audience — especially the students — were energized and motivated to ignite Selma's freedom movement.

As people walked to their parked cars, they discovered that the taillights had been smashed. The next day, police issued tickets to black people who were caught driving with a broken taillight.

On the night of June 11, Bernard saw two white men peering into the open hood of a car parked near his house. When he went over to help, he was bludgeoned in the head with a tire iron. Witnessing the attack, a neighbor charged out of his house with a gun, causing the assailants to flee.

Bernard spent the night in the hospital and was released the next morning. His face was covered with bruises, his eyes were swollen half shut, and his clothes were covered in blood. Rather than get cleaned up and change, he walked the downtown streets so everyone could see what had happened to him. When he returned home, he met Chuck, Terry, and Cleo, who were shocked at his appearance, but relieved he was alive.

Such was not the case for Medgar Evers, a beloved black NAACP freedom fighter in Jackson, Mississippi, who was Colia's friend and mentor. He was fatally gunned down outside his home hours after the attack on Bernard.

As terrifying as the assaults were to Chuck, they didn't discourage him or his fellow students. In fact, the brutal incidents gave them even more reason to keep pressing for change. "The whites will not stop us," he vowed.

Despite the risks, the students continued to canvass black neighborhoods, urging people to register to vote. On every registration day — which was held only twice a month — African Americans tried to register at the courthouse, but because of stalling tactics by county officials, only a few, if any, were able to sign up.

On September 15, 1963, Chuck was shaken to the core by the church bombing in Birmingham that snuffed out the lives of four innocent girls. In response, Chuck and his comrades led mass student demonstrations the next day in downtown Selma. At Carter's Drug Store, Chuck's friend Willie C. Robinson tried to place an order at the white lunch counter. He was bashed over the head with an ax handle by the owner, opening a gash that required seven stitches. The police wound up arresting four black students at the drug store, but not the assailant.

Over the next two weeks, more than 300 black students — including Chuck — were arrested for engaging in peaceful protests. Bettie Mae was upset by the events. "It's so unfair," she told Chuck. "Any white person can just walk up out of the crowd and do anything they want to a Negro, and nothing is done about it. But if we protest in any kind of way, we are immediately carried off to jail."

For the next voter registration day, October 7, 1963, SNCC leaders organized an all-out effort to get as many potential black voters as possible to the courthouse. They called it Freedom Day. By noon, more than 300 black persons were patiently and peacefully waiting in line, but only 12 had been allowed in the registrar's office to fill out the application.

Armed with clubs and electric cattle prods, 40 blue-helmeted state troopers looked for any excuse to arrest the black persons, many of whom were taunted by white onlookers. Mayor Joe Smitherman announced to the people standing in line, "If you leave the line for food, water, or the bathroom, you won't be allowed to rejoin. Nor will anyone be allowed to bring food or water to you."

Three SNCC members, including Chuck and Worth Long, stood on the steps of the federal building across the street from the courthouse, holding signs that read REGISTER TO VOTE. Sheriff Clark had them arrested and hauled off to jail for "unlawful assembly."

Although many in the black community were proud that they had stood up to the police for their right to register, Freedom Day proved costly for others. More than 40 black men and women lost their jobs and were put on a blacklist by the white citizens' council. That meant no white employer would hire them. As a result, there was plenty of resistance among the black adults to register because they knew their jobs were on the line. Chuck's sharecropping uncle in Crumptonia was terrified that he would be kicked off the farmland because Chuck was his nephew.

Chuck was undeterred. After the passage of the 1964 Civil Rights Act on July 2, he and his fellow leaders launched a series of sit-ins and demonstrations. To no one's surprise, they were met with stiff resistance.

During a sit-in at the Thirsty Boy drive-in, African Americans were attacked by whites — but the black demonstrators were the ones arrested on bogus charges of trespassing. At the movie theater, black people came down from the "colored" section — the balcony known as "the buzzard roost" — to the whites-only main floor only to get beaten up. The owner temporarily closed the theater rather than follow the new civil rights law.

The next night, SNCC held a mass meeting that attracted a big turnout. But Sheriff Clark labeled it "a riot" and squashed it by sending in 50 deputies and posse men with billy clubs and tear gas.

The following day, which was one of the two monthly voter registration days, SNCC chairman John Lewis led a column of black applicants to the courthouse. But Clark arrested them. As the African Americans were herded to jail, Clark and his men shocked them with cattle prods and jabbed them with billy clubs.

On July 9, Judge James Hare issued an injunction forbidding any gathering of three or more people involved in the civil rights movement. Chuck was on the list of leaders who weren't allowed to even talk to two or more people at the same time about voter registration in Selma. The injunction granted the judge the right to jail anyone he felt violated his order. That effectively stopped any demonstrations or mass meetings.

The movement in Selma faltered until the courts ruled that Hare's injunction was patently unconstitutional. Chuck began spending more time in the streets protesting than studying in the classroom. By his senior year in high school, he had been arrested a half dozen times. His grandmother often bailed him out, forking over $50 or $100 after each arrest, which was a lot of money for her.

By now the superintendent of the schools had instructed the principal of Chuck's high school to expel students who continued to demonstrate for civil rights. Although the decree slowed Chuck down, it didn't stop him. In fact, he and other students kept prodding teachers to register to vote. The teachers soon realized that it wasn't fair for them to remain on the sidelines while students risked expulsion and failure to graduate in their drive for civil rights for all.

On January 22, 1965, more than 100 teachers marched to the courthouse to register to vote. At the same time, Chuck and other SNCC leaders had packed two churches with hundreds of students who were poised to demonstrate if the teachers were harassed by the police. SNCC soon received a call reporting that the teachers had been turned away. "All right," Chuck told the students who had gathered inside First Baptist Church, "it's time they heard from us. Follow me."

Shoulder to shoulder, two by two, the students reached the center of town and blocked the courthouse entrance.

Sheriff Clark, his deputies, and posse men then surrounded the demonstrators.

Chuck stood in front of the scowling sheriff, who was wearing a helmet and armed with a gun, billy club, and cattle prod. After Clark ordered him to move, Chuck sang, *"Ain't gonna let Jim Clark turn me around, turn me around, turn me around. Ain't gonna let Jim Clark turn me around . . ."*

Clark took out his club and slapped it rhythmically against his hand as his angry face turned increasingly red. Then he began jabbing teachers and students. Following his lead, the deputies did, too, pushing people down the concrete steps. No mercy was shown to anyone — women and children were struck with billy clubs with the same ferocity reserved for the men.

But the demonstrators reformed their line and went back up the steps only to be knocked over like bowling pins. Refusing to quit, they tried a third time and suffered the same setback. Clark was screaming that he would arrest everyone. But then a district court judge told the fuming sheriff, "If you arrest all the teachers and students here, come Monday you'll have thousands more students running wild in the streets."

The protestors then headed for Brown Chapel, where well-wishers cheered them. Although no one was able to register to vote, Chuck noticed a change in attitude among the teachers. *They're no longer afraid,* he thought.

Over the next few weeks, African Americans carried out large but peaceful demonstrations that ended in their arrests, which totaled more than 1,800. Selma's jails were jammed beyond capacity, so many of the protestors were taken to outlying facilities, including Camp Selma, a state-run, chain-gang-style prison. It was so crowded the beds were removed, forcing inmates to sleep on the cold concrete floor. They had to drink from a common tub of water and use a single toilet. Their inedible, roach-infested meals typically consisted of black-eyed peas, a square of crumbly cornbread, a boiled chicken neck, and a cup of bitter black coffee.

During a demonstration on February 10, Clark, his deputies, and posse men forced students — some as young as nine — to run down a street and onto a road that led out of town. The kids who didn't move fast enough were clubbed or zapped by the cattle prods. Clark, riding in his car beside them, kept yelling, "Run! Faster! Faster!"

Some of the younger students collapsed from exhaustion or were vomiting and crying too hard to keep moving. The heartless posse men beat them. Finally, Clark and his men left, allowing the worn-out students to stagger home on their own.

"This is one more example of the inhuman, animal-like treatment of the Negro people of Selma, Alabama," SNCC leader John Lewis told the press afterward. "This nation has always come to the aid of people in foreign lands who are gripped by a reign of tyranny. Can this nation do less for the people of Selma?"

Frustrated by Alabama's refusal to grant voting rights to African Americans, hundreds of protestors agreed to march from Selma to the state capital in Montgomery — a distance of 50 miles — to confront Governor George Wallace. When he learned of their plans, Wallace forbade the march and ordered state troopers to "use whatever measures necessary" to prevent it.

Chuck and 600 others defied the governor and gathered outside Brown Chapel on the morning of March 7, 1965, a raw gray Sunday. Word spread that waiting for them at the city limits were Clark and his deputies, state troopers with tear gas, and posse men on horseback with whips. Chuck didn't know what to expect, but he had an uneasy feeling that this day would not end well.

The marchers — some dressed in their Sunday best — headed out, two by two, led by Lewis and Hosea Williams, a NAACP leader. Chuck was about ten rows from the front, walking with a newcomer from a Lutheran school who admitted he was nervous. "We all are," said Chuck. He sensed a collective fear among the somber demonstrators as they trekked silently toward the edge of town, marked by the arched Edmund Pettus Bridge.

When he reached the crest of the bridge, he saw a sight that jarred his nerves. On the other side of the Alabama River, more than 200 blue-helmeted state troopers and sheriff's deputies were lined three and four deep across the road. Dozens of squad cars were parked with their lights flashing. Off to the side, the hated posse men were joined by white thugs who were armed with bats and pipes and waving Confederate battle flags. White spectators, including mothers holding babies, lined the road behind them.

Although overwhelmed with fear, Chuck kept moving forward, knowing full well he was marching into hell. He stared at the cops' equipment — gas masks, guns, clubs, cattle prods, and long leather whips. *They have it all, and they're not going to let it go to waste,* he thought. *We're about to get beaten.*

When the first row of marchers came off the bridge, they were halted by a major for the state police. "This is an unlawful march," he announced through his bullhorn. "You can't go any farther. You have two minutes to turn around and disperse."

Lewis and Williams signaled to the marchers to kneel in prayer. Like the others, Chuck dropped to one knee. But he kept his head up, staring at the troopers who were now putting on their gas masks and pulling out their billy clubs. *Uh-oh, this is going to be bad.*

Seconds later, the major ordered, "Troopers, advance! Move in!"

The police charged into the first few rows of marchers, savagely bashing Lewis and Williams, who were knocked backward, semiconscious and bleeding. As the marchers fled in panic, the troopers broke ranks and flailed away, clubbing everyone in their path.

For a terrifying moment, Chuck didn't move. He heard people screaming in pain and horror. He heard the white spectators cheering and shouting, "Kill the niggers! Beat the niggers!" Then he heard what sounded like gunshots. Suddenly, he was shrouded in a cloud of smoke and began choking and coughing. *Tear gas!*

A tear gas canister had exploded at the feet of his marching partner, who was instantly overcome by the fumes and had collapsed. His lungs burning and eyes stinging, Chuck could barely breathe or see. Hacking and gasping, he blindly reached down and grabbed his partner and began dragging him away from the carnage. "We've . . . got to . . . get down . . . to the riverbank . . . and wash off . . . the gas," he wheezed.

But the posse men on horseback, bellowing rebel yells, galloped into the crowd to keep people from reaching the river. The attackers drove off the black protestors by lashing them with bullwhips, ropes, and rubber tubing wrapped in barbed wire. All the while, Chuck could hear Sheriff Clark shouting, "Get those damned niggers!" The cheers from the white spectators grew louder.

Barely able to catch his breath, Chuck threw his partner's arm around his neck and helped him return over the bridge while dodging and ducking the posse men and the brutes who were battering black people left and right. The tormentors pursued the marchers for nearly two miles back toward Brown Chapel. Any African American, whether a marcher or not, was now fair game for a beating at the hands of the out-of-control assailants.

Chuck stumbled along streets littered with people sprawling, crying, bleeding, and holding their heads. Some had been trampled by horses. When he finally arrived at the chapel, a posse man rode his horse up the church steps and began whipping people who were seeking sanctuary inside.

Chuck had bought into the philosophy of nonviolence. He had studied it and put it in practice. But this vicious police riot was too much to bear, and the urge to hurt someone had overtaken him. He wanted revenge. And he wanted it now.

His target was the posse man on horseback who had just lashed a boy with the whip, opening up a bloody head wound. Chuck picked up a brick and reared back, intent on hurling it at the horseman's head. But James Bevel, a SCLC leader who helped organize the march, gripped Chuck's arm, stopping him.

"Chuck, look at that kid on the ground," Bevel said. "See how his head is gashed open? Do you really want to do the same thing to that man on the horse?"

Given a few seconds to regain control of his emotions, Chuck shook his head and dropped the brick.

By the time Chuck and his marching partner made it into the chapel, it was swamped with wounded men, women, and children. About 100 of the 600 marchers required medical attention for fractured skulls, broken teeth and limbs, gas poisoning, and whip lashes.

The whiff of tear gas on the clothes and skin of victims lingered in the air. Chuck and other student leaders — their eyes puffy and breathing labored — tried to calm one another and offer support for those still numb from the brutality unleashed against them. Many were crying and hurting. Everyone was angry and dejected.

Chuck was crestfallen. *After all we've gone through — the beatings, the arrests, the jail time, the protests, and now this — Negroes here still can't register to vote.* He felt as if they were still being treated like slaves.

Before letting anyone take him to the hospital for treatment of his skull fracture, concussion, and head wounds, Lewis addressed his battered brothers and sisters in the chapel. "I don't know how President Johnson can send troops to Vietnam but he can't send troops to Selma, Alabama, to protect people whose only desire is to be able to vote," he said. "Next time we march, we may have to keep going beyond Montgomery. We may have to go all the way to Washington."

As evening approached on this day — which forever would be known as Bloody Sunday — the moaning and wailing that had been constant background noise in the chapel slowly died out. Then someone began humming a freedom song that quickly grew louder as others like Chuck joined in until everyone was humming it. Soon they began singing the tune, adding lyrics from the terrible events of the day: *"Ain't gonna let George Wallace turn me 'round . . . Ain't gonna let Jim Clark turn me 'round . . . Ain't gonna let no state trooper turn me 'round . . . Ain't gonna let no horses turn me 'round . . . Ain't gonna let no tear gas turn me 'round . . . Ain't gonna let nobody turn me 'round."*

Like everyone else in the chapel, Chuck could feel a renewed spirit burning in his soul. *Whatever it takes,* he told himself, *whatever suffering I have to face, I can handle it. I will not quit until we win the fight for equal rights. And one day we will win.*

Film and news accounts of Bloody Sunday shocked Americans, spurring many to get involved in the civil rights movement and hastening the passage of the Voting Rights Act of 1965.

Two days after the brutal attack, Chuck joined 2,000 other African Americans, 450 religious leaders from around the country, and various celebrities in another march, this one led by Dr. Martin Luther King, Jr., When they reached the Edmund Pettus Bridge, they were once again met by a huge police force. But there was no violence this time. After kneeling and praying, they returned to Brown Chapel.

On March 21, more than 3,200 people of all races, religions, and ages left Selma for a 4-day march to Montgomery, this time protected by the National Guard. When they arrived in Montgomery on March 25, they were joined by 25,000 demonstrators for a spirited rally in front of the Alabama State House.

Later, while attending Selma University, Chuck helped stage a student sit-in downtown even though the school had banned any student participation in the civil rights movement. For their actions, he and 39 fellow students were expelled. So Chuck then led a rally to protest the expulsions. Eventually, the school let all the students return — except for Chuck.

Devastated by his expulsion, Chuck went to California, where he attended City College of San Francisco and Sonoma State, and eventually earned a degree in anthropology while doing independent study in the African country of Tanzania for nearly two years. He returned to San Francisco, where he earned a law degree from New College School of Law at the same time his wife, Lorraine, earned a medical degree from Stanford. They set up their respective practices in the same office in Oakland. Today Charles (as he's now called) practices civil rights and personal injury law with his son Cabral at their firm, Bonner & Bonner, in Sausalito, California.

Despite more than 40 arrests and many physical attacks and serious injuries, John Lewis has remained a devoted advocate of the philosophy of nonviolence. He has been serving in Congress since 1987 as a United States representative from Georgia and remains one of the country's most respected civil rights leaders.

Bernard Lafayette, Jr., who was arrested more than two dozen times, became an ordained Baptist minister and served as president of the American Baptist Theological Seminary. A founder of the Center for Nonviolence & Peace Studies at the University of Rhode Island, he is recognized as one of the world's leading experts on nonviolent direct action.

ABOUT THE AUTHOR

Allan Zullo is the author of more than 100 nonfiction books on subjects ranging from sports and the supernatural to history and animals.

He has introduced Scholastic readers to the Ten True Tales series, gripping stories of extraordinary persons who have met the challenges of dangerous, sometimes life-threatening, situations. Among the books in the series are *FBI Heroes, Heroes of 9/11, Heroes of the Vietnam War, World War I Heroes, World War II Heroes, War Heroes: Voices from Iraq,* and *Battle Heroes: Voices from Afghanistan.* In addition, he has authored four books about the real-life experiences of young people during the Holocaust — *Survivors: True Stories of Children in the Holocaust, Heroes of the Holocaust: True Stories of Rescues by Teens, Escape: Children of the Holocaust,* and *We Fought Back: Teen Resisters of the Holocaust.*

Allan, the father of two grown daughters and grand-father of five, lives with his wife, Kathryn, near Asheville, North Carolina. To learn more about the author, visit his website at www.allanzullo.com.